Commitment to Sust<

Ooligan Press is committed to be
an academic leader in sustainable publishing
practices. Using both the classroom and the
business, we will investigate, promote, and
utilize sustainable products, technologies, and
practices as they relate to the production and
distribution of our books. We hope to lead
and encourage the publishing community by
our example. Making sustainable choices is
not only vital to the future of our industry—
it's vital to the future of our world.

OpenBook Series

One component of our sustainability campaign is the OpenBook
Series. *Rethinking Paper & Ink: The Sustainable Publishing Revolution*
is the fifth book in the series, so named to highlight our
commitment to transparency on our road toward sustainable
publishing. We believe that disclosing the impacts of the choices
we make will not only help us avoid unintentional greenwashing,
but also serve to educate those who are unfamiliar with the choices
available to printers and publishers.

Efforts to produce this series as sustainably as possible focus
on paper and ink sources, design strategies, efficient and safe
manufacturing methods, innovative printing technologies,
supporting local and regional companies, and corporate responsibility of our contractors.

All titles in the OpenBook Series will have the OpenBook logo
on the front cover and a corresponding OpenBook Environmental
Audit inside, which includes a calculated paper impact from the
Environmental Defense Fund.

Figures below relate to a print run of 2,000 books	Chemicals	Greenhouse Gases

Paper[†]

Cover paper: 100-lb. Mohawk Loop Silk, 50% PCW, FSC®-certified, manufactured by Mohawk Fine Papers in Hamilton, OH. 172 lbs. used.

.05-lb. reduction of VOCs; .07-lb. reduction of HAPs. [§]

88.14-lb. reduction of CO_2 equivalent. [§]

Text paper: 60-lb. Harbor 100 Offset, 100% PCW, PCF, FSC-certified, manufactured by Grays Harbor Paper in Hoquaim, WA. 1,903 lbs. used.

3-lb. reduction of VOCs; 3-lb. reduction of HAPs.[§]

2,341-lb. reduction of CO_2 equivalent.[§]

Printing & Binding

Covers printed on a Heidelberg Speedmaster SM52-6+L 6 color press and interiors printed on a Heidelberg Speedmaster 102-6(P) 6 color press by Hemlock Printers in Vancouver, BC.

Hemlock uses Saphira Bio Press Wash (manufactured by Heidelberg) to clean press equipment.

Saphira Bio Press Wash contains less than 10% VOCs.

Perfect bound with IFS Dural PUR. Approx. 9 lbs. used.

Polyurethane adhesives are not water-soluble, meaning they are easier to remove during recycling than adhesives like ethylene vinyl acetate (EVA).

Insufficient data.

Covers finished with an aqueous coating manufactured by Coating & Adhesive in Leland, NC. Approx. 3 lbs. used.

Insufficient data.

Aqueous coatings reduce VOC emissions since they are water-based instead of petroleum-based.

Ink

Supertech 520 manufactured by Superior Printing Ink based in Teterboro, NJ. Approx. 8 lbs. used.

Supertech 520 is 23-30% vegetable based and has no petroleum content.

Supertech 520 contains approximately 5% VOCs.

The OpenBook Audit—performed by Ooligan Press—stems from our commitment to transparency in our efforts to produce a line of books using the most sustainable materials and processes available to us. All quantities and material specifications supplied by Hemlock Printers.

Energy	Fiber	Waste
290,000 BTU reduction in net energy [§]; Mohawk Loop Silk is manufactured with windpower and is carbon neutral.	0.13-ton reduction in virgin fiber use, the equivalent of about 0.93 trees.[§]	25.77-lb. reduction in solid waste; 424.52-gal. waste-water reduction.[§]
8 million BTU reduction in net energy.[§]	4-ton reduction in virgin fiber use, the equivalent of about 25 trees.[§]	684-lb. reduction in solid waste; 11,273-gal. waste-water reduction.[§]
Hemlock is a carbon neutral company that sources renewable energy for their operations and invests in carbon offsetting through Offsetters.	Hemlock recycled all make-ready (including paper and other substrates) left over from print runs.	Hemlock also recycles all plates and metal materials used during print jobs and over 90% of plastics, rags, solvents, wastewater, inks, batteries, and compostables.
Insufficient data.	Insufficient data.	Insufficient data.
Insufficient data.	Insufficient data.	Insufficient data.
Insufficient data.	N/A	Insufficient data.

[†]Environmental impact estimates were made using the EDF Paper Calculator tool at http://www.papercalculator.org.
[§] Compared to paper made with 100% virgin fiber.

Offsetting This Book

by **Hemlock Printers** *www.hemlock.com/zero*

While *Rethinking Paper & Ink* takes advantage of available products and processes to reduce its environmental impact, there are still carbon emissions that stem from the transportation and manufacturing of each element of the book's print run. To offset all emissions produced by the book's print run, we have opted to take part in *Zero*, Hemlock's Carbon Neutral Printing Program.

Zero makes up for carbon emissions during paper production and transportation from the fiber's source to the paper mill, and from there to the printer. Hemlock calculates a print run's carbon emissions in two steps. First, they determine the emissions released in sourcing and producing the paper stock using the Environmental Defense Fund's Paper Calculator. Next, transportation-related emissions are calculated with the Greenhouse Gas Protocol Transportation Tool.

These offsets are offered through a partnership with Offsetters, an organization that invests in renewable energy and clean technology. All of these offsets are verified by a third party against the ISO 14064-2—a specification on quantifying, monitoring, and reporting greenhouse gas emissions—and meet the Gold Standard of the UN Framework Convention on Climate Change. Since 2005, Offsetters has offset over 275,000 tons of carbon emissions

Praise for *Rethinking Paper & Ink*

"*Rethinking Paper & Ink: The Sustainable Publishing Revolution* is a fantastic follow-up to its predecessor. [Ooligan Press], this time, delves deeper into the publishing industry's environmental impacts…However, *Rethinking Paper & Ink* doesn't just focus on the problem—it provides practical options to help remedy the crisis…[It] ensure[s] that the reading audience understands that sustainability is a moving target that evolves with technology and global events. It is important… to keep aware, educated, and [be] willing to try new avenues in book publishing in order to keep this industry alive and moving forward in this century and beyond."

—*Eric Benson, Partner, Re-nourish*

"When I heard about a book called *Rethinking Paper & Ink*, my first thought was: "Hey, that's also what we do with our Ecofont software!" While reading the book, I was amazed by the diversity of both smart ideas and workable solutions. All this rethinking can really make a difference in the use of paper and ink. Moreover, the book shows that the ongoing changes in our world ask for constant rethinking on the way we approach things. An inspiring book."

—*Gerjon Zomer, Co-founder, EcoFont/Spranq*

"*Rethinking Paper & Ink* is the first truly comprehensive assessment of the book publishing industry's environmental impact. As publishers grapple with how to make publishing a more sustainable enterprise, this is a superb, must-read resource."

—*Margo Baldwin, President and Publisher, Chelsea Green*

Rethinking Paper & Ink
THE SUSTAINABLE PUBLISHING REVOLUTION

Jessicah Carver & Natalie Guidry
Ooligan Press • Portland, Oregon • 2011

OOLIGAN
PRESS

Rethinking Paper & Ink: The Sustainable Publishing Revolution
©2010 Ooligan Press
Portland State University

ISBN 978-1-932010-39-8

Library of Congress Cataloging-in-Publication Data

Carver, Jessicah.
Rethinking paper & ink : the sustainable publishing revolution / Jessicah Carver and Natalie Guidry.
   p. cm. — (OpenBook)
New and expanded ed. of: Rethinking paper and ink / Melissa Brumer. 2009.
Summary: "Rethinking Paper & Ink offers a critical examination of the book publishing industry and discusses ways to achieve more sustainable practices. Through extensive research and experience in the industry, the authors present ideas on sustainability within the book-making process, reviewing the environmental impacts of acquisitions and editing, design and printing, marketing and distribution, and both print and digital sales. Rethinking Paper & Ink includes a detailed account of the choices Ooligan Press made to produce the book itself and features industry profiles that highlight remarkable individuals, organizations, and businesses exemplifying these standards"— Provided by publisher.
Includes bibliographical references and index.
ISBN 978-1-932010-39-8 (pbk.)
   1. Publishers and publishing—Environmental aspects. 2. Book industries and trade—Environmental aspects. 3. Publishers and publishing—Environmental aspects—United States. 4. Book industries and trade—Environmental aspects—United States. 5. Sustainable development. I. Guidry, Natalie. II. Brumer, Melissa. Rethinking paper and ink. III. Title. IV. Title: Rethinking paper and ink.
   Z278.C325 2011
   070.5—dc22
                                 2011002576

Cover art and design by Brian David Smith
Interior design by Kerri Higby and Brian David Smith

Ooligan Press
Department of English
Portland State University
PO Box 751, Portland, Oregon 97207
503.725.9748 (phone); 503.725.3561 (fax)
ooligan@ooliganpress.pdx.edu
http://www.ooliganpress.pdx.edu
Printed in Canada

Contents

Authors' Note

Rethinking Paper & Ink: The Sustainable Publishing Revolution began as a booklet published in March 2009 by Ooligan Press. Melissa Brumer and Janine Eckhart, graduate students in the Master's in Writing/Book Publishing program at Portland State University and the founders of Ooligan's Sustainable Publishing Initiative, started researching sustainable book publishing and were unable to find any books specifically focused on the subject. This absence made them realize there was a general need for one in the market. They applied for and received a grant from the James F. and Marion L. Miller Foundation to fund the printing of "a sustainable book about sustainable bookmaking." Per the terms of the Miller Grant, the booklet (printed locally by Pinball Publishing, with an initial print run of 1,000 copies) was free of charge, and Ooligan Press additionally provided a free PDF of the book on its website to increase accessibility. The project was met with great interest and within a few months it became apparent that a reprint would be necessary. During preliminary discussions about this reprint, it was decided that an expanded and updated version would be the most responsible way to continue the life of this project.

Ooligan Press decided to acquire *Rethinking Paper & Ink* as a full-length title in its catalog. We saw a trade book as an opportunity to reach a broader national audience with our distributor and explore options that weren't possible with the first booklet. At this point, in late fall of 2009, we had begun co-managing the Sustainable Production department at Ooligan Press, which oversees the OpenBook Series and functions as the environmental conscience of every aspect of the press. We decided that writing this book would allow us to dive deeply into research and become more integrated into the field of sustainable publishing, so we outlined a proposal for the expansion of Melissa and Janine's original booklet. During ensuing meetings with Dennis Stovall, Ooligan's publisher, and Abbey Gaterud, the assistant publisher, it was decided that the two of us would write the full length, expanded version of the original *Rethinking Paper & Ink*.

Over the next year, we researched, wrote, talked with leaders in the industry, and got involved in the larger sustainability community. We had the opportunity to present some of our work on sustainable publishing at AIGA's Shift: A Green Design Salon and also at the "Sustainability in Art and New Media" panel at Portland Center for Public Humanities' Understanding Sustainability Conference.

Although this book doesn't have nearly enough space to comprehensively cover every aspect of the current book industry and sustainability, we hope it functions as a critical examination of book publishing and offers positive, viable sustainable alternatives to continue inspiring change and growth. One thing this book will *not* do is be a how-to guide with formulaic advice on how to achieve sustainable publishing. Sustainability should not be thought of as an end goal, but as an evolving process and way of thinking. The current publishing industry employs varying degrees of environmentally friendly practices and materials. The goals of this book are to start an informative discourse with best practices in mind and to present the information we've gathered in an accessible manner for anyone interested in these topics. We want publishing professionals, sustainability advocates, and the everyday book lover to use it as a tool to help them make the most responsible decisions possible in their operations, advocacy, and reading choices.

We hope that this book offers an informative contribution to the ongoing discussion of the role of sustainability in book publishing. As ardent bibliophiles who genuinely acknowledge the value of the book and are invested in its future (as both a printed artifact and in digital forms), we feel it's necessary for us to continue this dialog and invite others to consider the nuances of what it means to responsibly produce books. One of the most pleasurable aspects of creating this book was to write the industry profiles, which highlight some of the remarkable individuals, organizations, and businesses that we feel exemplify the standards we discuss. Although some of the information in this book might seem dismal, we hope that each reader walks away from it inspired by everyone in the industry who works hard to effect change, and be encouraged by all the exciting possibilities before us.

We certainly couldn't have written this book alone. Our enormous gratitude goes out to Dennis Stovall, Abbey Gaterud, Melissa Brumer, Janine Eckhart, Alyson Hoffman, Molly Woods, Kjerstin Johnson, Kerri Higby, Brian Smith, and all the other amazing individuals at Ooligan Press who made this book possible. We also want to profusely thank our families and friends, without whose love and support we couldn't have come this far.

—Jessicah Carver *&* Natalie Guidry

Introduction

triple bottom line | A method of measuring overall performance based on the economic, environmental, and social performances of a business, rather than the traditional single bottom line approach, which only considers economic factors.

SUSTAINABLE DEVELOPMENT:
Using human and natural resources to meet human needs in a way that does not jeopardize the needs of future generations.

BOOK PUBLISHING: *The process of making literature and information available for public view. This process includes: acquisition, copyediting, design, production, printing (and its electronic equivalents), marketing, and the sales and distribution of books.*

This book is about incorporating sustainable practices into the book publishing industry. While "sustainability" may be an overused term, the concept is always relevant, though commonly misunderstood. At Ooligan Press, sustainability means **triple bottom line** thinking. This book asks: How can we design and implement a book publishing system—from concept to consumer—that is sustainable not only financially, but also socially and environmentally? Because of resource restraints, this book mainly focuses on the environmental impacts of book publishing. Deeper issues, such as creating an adaptive publishing system complete with indicators and metrics to track success, are extremely important and briefly addressed in this introduction.

About Sustainability, Indicators, and Metrics

The model below represents a general view of sustainability. The spheres correlate to the three components of the triple bottom line.

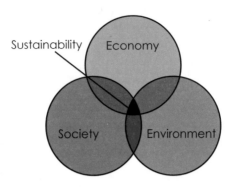

Society, the environment, and the economy are represented as equal and separate entities. The area of overlap is where sustainable development occurs.

This is the model we prefer:

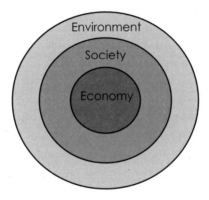

Here, society is contained within the environment, and the economy is contained within society—the smaller spheres of society and economy are non-existent without the larger sphere of environment.

Economy

Is the current economic system sustainable for society and the environment? Or does it lead to the consumption and degradation of the environment and create larger disparities in income and well-being, eventually leading to its own demise? Indicators such as **Gross Domestic Product** (GDP) and other less conventional tools of measurement such as the **Happy Planet Index** (HPI) exist to measure economic and social health.[1] But the idea of using GDP as a measurement for total well-being is flawed. It ignores issues of equity (income distribution) as well as quality of life, and it says nothing about environmental impacts. This is why economists and social scientists have tried to create indicators that capture the larger context—and true impacts—of our economic system, such as HPI. The Happy Planet Index accounts for factors such as life expectancy, life satisfaction, and ecological footprint, then compares the data to per capita GDP in order to understand whether the economic growth reflected is outweighed by other social and environmental costs.

Society

Social sustainability is about equity. A high standard of life for a small percentage of the world's population (the "developed world") at the cost of environmental quality and social well-being for a larger percentage of the world's population (the "developing world") is not an equitable, efficient, effective, or sustainable method of development. The United Nation's **Human Development Index** (HDI) measures whether the basic needs of people are being met.[2] HDI compares life expectancy and child mortality rates, literacy rates and the percentage of children enrolled in school, and the purchasing power of individuals (per capita GDP). The **Gini coefficient** measures distribution of income, showing where approximate income equality exists in the world, by country.[3] These types of measurements typically look at: material living standards (consumption and wealth), health, education, personal activities

Happy Planet Index (HPI) | Created by the New Economics Foundation (NEF) in 2006, this is a response to indices such as GDP and HDI, which do not take sustainability into account. The basic assumption of the HPI is that socio-economic growth should reflect the goal of an achievable level of happiness and health for the most people, and that the environmental costs of pursuing those goals are taken into account.

Human Development Index (HDI) | A measurement created to address the false presumption of the GDP: that national economic growth is synonymous with human welfare. (*See glossary for more.*)

Gini coefficient | Developed in 1912, this measurement is used in sustainability to determine social inequalities such as income distribution. The Gini coefficient is a value ranging from 0 (total equality of distribution) to 1 (total inequality of distribution).

indicator species | A species so closely associated with an ecosystem that its presence or absence is indicative of the health of that ecosystem.

biodiversity | The concept of measuring the health of an ecosystem by considering the amount of variable life forms within it. A significant negative factor, which affects a system's biodiversity, is extinction of a species through direct removal (e.g., clear-cutting a specific species of tree for wood fiber) or indirect removal (e.g., removing an animal's necessary food source).

panarchy | The concept that ecosystems and social-ecosystems exist in hierarchies of cycles that adapt to changes. (*See glossary for more.*)

best practices | The processes, practices, and systems that allow for the most desirable outcome for a given industry.

human capital | This refers to the stock of talents, knowledge, and capabilities that individuals contribute to the process of the production of goods and services.

(including work), political voice and governance, social connections and relationships, environmental quality, transportation and housing options, and personal security. When we talk about social sustainability, these are the issues we refer to.

Environment

The environmental issues associated with the concept of sustainability are the issues people are most familiar with. Perhaps the reason for this is that measurable environmental impacts of a given choice or behavior are the most visible. These impacts are monitored by measuring toxin accumulation, observing the health and behaviors of wildlife (especially **indicator species**), studying climate changes, and measuring the health of the different functions of ecosystem services. **Biodiversity** is a very important element of sustainability. According to the theory of **panarchy**, the more diverse a system is, the more adaptive it is. The more resilient it is to disturbances, the more sustainable it is.[4]

Both metrics and indicators are vital for tracking environmental successes and failures. The publishers at Ooligan Press have implemented an audit system to track its progress toward sustainable publishing, and maintain integrity through transparent decision-making and processes. All of the books in the OpenBook Series, a collection of books published using the **best practices** and sustainable processes, include an audit within the first few pages of the book. The audit is the press's first step toward an inclusive system of sustainability monitoring and reporting.

How does book publishing fit into this broader view of sustainability? Book publishing is the process of making literature and information available for public view. The value added by this process can be found in the economic and social spheres—books are educational tools and have great potential to increase **human capital** and well-being. At the global level, books are arguably the most equally accessible mediums of information transfer. As publishers, we have options in acquisition, design, and production to ensure that the costs of the publishing process do not outweigh the benefits. Is the environmental consumption and degradation worth the amount of human capital and well-being that is created? It's not an easy question to answer given that we don't have metrics or information to compare all the relevant variables. Things like clean air, water, and education are impossible to assign a value to.

The industrial revolution was an era driven by ideas of indefinite growth. We are, however, at a point in human history at which those industrial-age systems need to be reassessed. The rate of growth that those systems perpetuate is neither necessary for human survival nor sustainable. One model of sustainable design, the **cradle to cradle** (c2c) model, acknowledges that all systems on the planet are **interdependent**, and that there is no waste in nature. The cradle to cradle model provides a framework for living within the environment in a way that has a neutral impact.

To achieve sustainability, shifts are needed in the policies and infrastructures that drive the publishing industry. These shifts are large in scale: reallocating government subsidies to create financial incentives for businesses to make sustainable choices, restructuring the economy to properly value intangibles like human welfare and **ecosystem services** like

cradle to cradle (c2c) | An approach in design. Rather than designing an object from the cradle to grave approach (that is, for a single use), designing it with recycling or reuse in mind, so that the quality of the material can withstand a large or indefinite number of recycling processes. The sustainability of an object or process starts with the design.

interdependence | The dynamic relationships between all living things and the systems in which those things exist; these are relationships of mutual dependence for the success or survival of each individual constituent and of the whole unit.

ecosystem services | The products and services provided by ecosystems that benefit humans and are necessary for a healthy planet. Examples include: food, water, timber, carbon sequestration, oxygen production, water purification, pollination, and nutrient cycling, as well as recreational, aesthetic, and spiritual benefits.

carbon sequestration| A term that describes the process of removing carbon dioxide from the atmosphere. Carbon sequestration can occur artificially or naturally, through biological, chemical, and physical processes. Photosynthesis is an example of a natural biochemical process of carbon sequestration.

carbon sequestration, and developing effective regulations in commerce. For sustainable development to be integrated into any industry, both large- and small-scale issues must be addressed simultaneously.

Using the intelligence of natural systems, the cradle to cradle model helps create smaller-scale industrial systems that are resourceful and efficient. For example, when a tree sprouts (cradle) and then dies (transition), it decomposes and releases nutrients that support new life systems (back to cradle). But in book publishing, we take raw materials from the earth (cradle), and in the process of making literature and information available, we degrade the environment (transition). In the end, the majority of energy and the materials, such as paper and ink, end up as waste (grave).

By employing a cradle to cradle model, identifying indicators, and defining metrics specific to the publishing industry, it is possible for publishers to help redesign the system in a way that allows books to have a neutral or even positive impact.

Of the three spheres (Environment, Society, and Economy), this book will focus on the largest—the Environment—without which the other two, as we know them, do not exist. The goal of *Rethinking Paper & Ink* is to provide information about the environmental impacts of publishing so that informed decisions can be made at the corporate and individual level. There is no single formula for producing a sustainable book. Technologies are forever changing; the best thing to do is to stay educated, stay motivated, and adapt behaviors appropriately.

—Melissa Brumer

Co-Founder of Ooligan Press's Sustainable Publishing Initiative and OpenBook Series

A great change in our stewardship of the earth and the life on it is required, if vast human misery is to be avoided and our global home on this planet is not to be irretrievably mutilated.

—World Scientists' Warning to Humanity (1992)

Some 1,700 of the world's leading scientists, including the majority of Nobel laureates in the sciences, issued this appeal in November 1992. The World Scientists' Warning to Humanity was written and spearheaded by the late Henry Kendall, former chair of the Union of Concerned Scientists' board of directors.

PART I: A Book's Life

Each person has his or her own book-shopping experiences—seeking out a recommendation from the owner of a local bookstore, browsing bestsellers while grabbing a cup of coffee, taking a chance on a yellow-paged novel found in the back of a favorite used bookstore, or clicking "Add to Cart" online. A book buyer might wonder whether the latest political pundit's book is really worth fifteen dollars, what caused his or her favorite short story author to produce such a shoddy first novel, or what expression a friend's face will have when they receive a book of poems as a gift. However, people usually don't think about how the book was made, where the paper came from, what kind of coating graces the cover, or how the purchase impacts the environment. The truth is, behind the glossy cover of romance novels or the crisp design of a coffee table book is an entire system of production and distribution. Accurately assessing traditional book publishing practices to determine how more responsible, sustainable actions might be taken requires examining every aspect of this system.

A Book's Life in a Publishing House

To begin, books you find at a bookstore have taken a complex journey and have traveled quite a distance to arrive there. Once the author has written the proposal or completed the manuscript, she begins pitching her story to agents or directly to publishing houses. In the past, authors went straight to editors at publishing houses. But as publishers got bigger, it became harder for the author to reach the editor directly. As a result, agents "increasingly became the writer's primary point of contact with the publishing world," particularly because "most editors and publishers [didn't] want to negotiate financial and contractual details with authors."[5] This is where the agent, as an advocate for the author's best interests in the negotiation process, comes in. Agents know what publishers are looking for, and often work closely with authors to shape their projects before presenting them to publishers. But not every author is able, or even interested in, working with an agent, so many unpublished authors send their manuscripts directly to publishers (a process called querying). Once a publishing house decides to acquire a title, they work with the author—or agent—on a contract outlining the terms of publication, **royalties**, and the **subsidiary rights** of the book (which might include electronic rights, movie and television rights, audio book rights, audiovisual rights, merchandising rights, and dramatic or performance rights).

Every press works on a different schedule, and even within a publishing house some books are given greater priority than others, but this is rarely a quick process. After the contract is solidified, the book goes through varying degrees of editing, which could include developing the story and characters, copyediting, proofreading, indexing, and typecoding. Meanwhile, other departments within the publishing house work on the book's cover and interior design, and gear its sales, marketing, and publicity operations toward the book. Long before the book is printed, the publisher is working with its distributor (or, less often, it might have its own in-house sales team and independent distribution system) to line up sales prior to the book's release. These sales are made with bookstores (individual independents or regional chains), but also with other sales venues like big box stores (Wal-Mart, Target, Costco), specialty stores, airports, libraries, and online retailers like Amazon.

Eventually the book is ready to be produced. Publishers don't do the actual production in-house. Almost always a book is sent to an outside printer who specializes in book printing. The impacts of this phase in the production of a book are analyzed in more detail in Part II. After a book is printed, it must get to the consumer, and that process is more complicated than it may appear.

A Book's Life After the Publishing House

Publishers rarely sell books directly to retailers. They contract with distributors, a third-party company that functions as the publisher's external sales force, stocking and actively selling books through sales representatives to bookstores. Distributors most often stock titles on consignment, and the majority of retailers buy from a distributor because of the ease of use and the ease of bookkeeping. The book distribution system was developed to make it easier for bookstores to get the books they wanted to sell. Rather than placing a dozen orders with a dozen publishers for a couple copies of a book, a bookstore buyer can place one order with a distributor, get one shipment, and pay for shipping just once. The distributor's sales reps deal with booksellers directly and may specialize in certain types of books or regions of the country. They stay abreast of new books, trends, and the changing interests of readers.

After they are printed, the books are transported (via truck, train, plane, or boat) to the distributor's warehouse, and then shipped to myriad bookstores and distribution centers across the country (and then possibly back again, as will be discussed later). A **wholesaler** is essentially a warehouse, and ships books to anyone with a retail license, but does not market or sell books for a publisher. Wholesalers, like distributors, make it easier for bookstores to order a variety of titles from one vendor, but they are also customers themselves. Often wholesalers will buy directly from a distributor and have the books shipped from one warehouse (the distributor's) to another (the wholesaler's), increasing the travel distance and **carbon footprint** of an individual book. As shown in Table 1, emissions related to the physical transportation of books and the energy used by storage facilities and bookstores make up 12.7% of a book's overall environmental impact, a calculation that doesn't account for direct-to-consumer or online sales, which are likely higher due to individual packaging and shipments.

Table 1. Carbon Impact Areas for the U.S. Book Industry[6]

Segments of the Industry	Share of Carbon Emissions	Notes
Forest & Forest Harvest Impacts	62.7%	Harvest and transport of fiber to the mill constitute only 1.52%; the remainder, 61.22%, is removal of biomass from the forest. A portion of the latter is offset by storage in books, recycling of books, and energy recovery.
Paper Production, Printing Impacts	26.6%	Paper production at the mill constitutes 22.4%; the remainder, 4.16%, is from printing and binding.
Distribution & Retail Impacts	12.7%	Distribution is for books to the market; retail is energy consumed by stores.
Landfill Releases	8.2%	Amount of methane released from books discarded in landfills.
Publishers' Impacts	6.6%	Publishers' impacts are energy used in offices, internal paper consumption, and business travel.
Carbon in Books & Energy Recovery	-16.8%	Books store a portion of the carbon from biomass in the products themselves; incinerating waste, although it has some of its own environmental risks, recovers some energy.

Even the packaging of books comes at an environmental cost. Books are transported in cardboard boxes that may not efficiently accommodate large or abnormally shaped books. If the book has certain design elements, such as flaps or extensive die cutting, it may require the additional protection of individual shrink-wrapping, which is generally sourced from nonrenewable petroleum. Books sold through online or other direct-to-consumer sales are repackaged into individual boxes before shipment, requiring more resources and potentially adding to landfill accumulation.

Books that don't end up reaching a reader through retail sales—the books not purchased—have another story. In trade publishing, "a book has just a few weeks—typically no more than six, and in practice often less—to show whether it's going to move, and if it's not moving then it will be pulled out of promotions."[7] Unsold titles might then be either recycled or returned to the publisher, where they can be sold to the author, donated, pulped, **remaindered**, or stored in a warehouse. Keep in mind that booksellers often overstock—ordering more books than they expect to sell—which means some books might be shipped to and from bookstores without even getting time on the shelf.

Overstocking is a common practice because bookstores can usually return unsold books for a complete refund, which is called the "right of return" in the industry. The right of return was established during the Great Depression of the 1930s when bookstores became more conservative in their purchasing. They started to stock fewer and fewer titles, and usually only those by well-known authors, books that were almost guaranteed to sell. Publishers—beginning with Putnam, Norton, and Knopf in the spring of 1930[8]—agreed to sell books on consignment simply to get their books in front of the customer. Having books on the shelf was the only way their books were going to sell (there were

remaindered book | A book that is not selling. A publisher sells it on a nonreturnable basis at a large discount. The publisher takes a loss on each copy sold as a remainder, but recovers a little of the initial investment and clears space in the warehouse. The overproduction of books and unpredictability, or overestimation, of sales greatly increases a book's chance of becoming a remainder.

very few other sales avenues at the time) and publishers needed to sell books in order to invest in new titles and authors. For publishers, sending bookstores the newest titles without pre-payment at least gave them a chance. For bookstores, ordering books no longer carried any financial risk because they could always return the books without penalty. This practice of returns is quite unique to the book industry and is unusual in broader retail sectors. This custom of returning unsold resalable copies to the publishers for full credit is one that publishers have since integrated into their business models, but have come to loathe for many reasons. The waste of resources is impractical in an industry already working with tight profit margins and overworked employees. It was a practical solution during the Great Depression, but over the last seventy years the publishing business model has evolved, as has the technology used to track the model, and yet book sales and distribution practices remain the same, never evolving to adapt more efficiently to the shifting landscape.

Directly related to the right of return is the fact that publishers typically print more books than they will (or can) actually sell. Publishers (through their distributors and wholesalers) sell a certain number of books to retailers, but retailers will usually return a percentage of the books they ordered under the right of return (this percentage fluctuates by title, but the industry average hovers around 30%[9]) making it necessary to print more than needed simply to fulfill the first round of orders. Though the majority of the print run's cost comes from paper, the percentage of total cost coming from set-up charges declines with more printed copies. This lowers the unit cost per book as the print run increases. If a publisher believes a book will sell between eight and ten thousand copies in the first several years of its life, often they will print the higher number because the unit cost of the book will be lower and they believe all copies of the print run will eventually sell. But, as we've discussed, that doesn't always happen.

Booksellers can also redeem *damaged* books for a refund. Mass-market paperbacks, like genre fiction (romance, sci-fi, westerns), are sometimes stripped of their front covers if they have not sold. The bookseller ships the covers to the publisher as proof of unsold and damaged books for their refund, and typically disposes of the main portion of the books in dumpsters. With mass-market paperbacks, the book object has such little monetary value to the publisher that it's not even worth it to restock it for a second sale. It's of little comfort that these dumpster-bound books cut back on the shipping emissions of regular returns, as a landfill destination renders the book's entire production cycle a wasteful one.

Books that end up in landfills not only reduce a valuable source for recycled paper fiber, but also contribute to the emissions of **greenhouse gases**. Paper waste generates a significant amount of landfill contributions, comprising roughly 31% of all municipal solid waste in the United States in 2008.[10] Out of the 78 million tons of paper goods discarded, only 55% were recovered for recycling.[11] The natural decomposition of paper in landfills leads to **methane** emissions through **anaerobic processes**. Methane is a greenhouse gas that remains in the atmosphere for nine to fifteen years and is twenty times more effective at trapping heat in the atmosphere than **carbon dioxide**.[12] Landfill emissions are the largest contribution to methane emissions in the United States, making up 34% of all methane emissions.[13]

According to standard economic valuations, once someone goes home with a purchased book, the sale is considered a success. Financially, the consumer has supported the publisher and retailer, allowing them to continue to publish future titles. However, examining the scenario from the triple bottom line perspective provides additional dimensions to the transaction. Ideally, the sale of a book provides positive financial gain, which could fuel a

greenhouse gases (GHG) | Gases in the Earth's atmosphere that are linked to global warming as they trap in the heat from the sun by absorption and emission of radiation. GHGs include carbon dioxide, ozone, methane, nitrous oxide, and water vapor.

carbon dioxide (CO_2) | A gas that is released from the combustion of organic matter. It can occur naturally through the carbon cycle or through man-made emissions, such as burning fossil fuels. Carbon dioxide emissions are the most commonly measured greenhouse gas emissions and are typically associated with climate change.

more sustainable production cycle of future titles. Environmentally, the sale of a book prevents all production impacts from being squandered on an unused product. Sold books also have the potential to increase human capital by extending the cultural and educational benefits of the information shared within them. Many people would agree that by reading a book, the reader is enriching his or her mind, which is one argument for ensuring that the environmental impacts of its production aren't wasted.

It is the book left unsold on the shelf that fails both frameworks. Not only is it an economic waste, as the standard framework would say, the value of an unsold book is considerably lower than that of a sold book in the triple bottom line framework. An unsold book's negative environmental impacts stem from landfill emissions or, if recycled, the necessary energy to turn the paper into pulp. By not reaching its audience, the unsold book cannot contribute to society in any educational or cultural manner.

Looking Forward

Millions of books go unsold every year. This fact reflects complicated problems deeply entrenched in an antiquated and outdated system. The book publishing industry (including distribution and sales) has major problems and weaknesses, and is in many ways nonsensical, perpetuating unsustainable practices. The impact on the environment due to waste and emissions from packaging and transporting books across the world is a problem with no easy solution, but there are ways to change this system, some of which are achievable in the short-term, some of which are long-term, industry-wide issues that will take a monumental movement to address. Overhauling the entire distribution system would do a lot to alleviate these issues, but such an overhaul would need to include improved methods by Barnes & Noble and Borders Group, Inc., currently the two largest bookstore chains in the United States, and big retail chains like Wal-Mart and Costco. Because these companies control such a large portion of the industry sales, smaller and independent publishers and bookstores may be unable to enforce widespread changes in the distribution process until changes are made by the larger companies. Until then, it's difficult to imagine a radical alleviation of the detrimental effects of current distribution practices. However, small changes can be implemented to reduce the harm of these practices.

A **Print on Demand** (POD) model can be a viable alternative for the printing and distribution of titles that are not in high demand but should still be accessible to the public. The small digital presses used in this process are capable of producing single or multiple books as they are ordered, and present an attractive alternative to large print runs, particularly for smaller publishing houses. In less than ten minutes, these book-making machines can print, bind, and trim a paperback book that boasts a full-color cover and quality almost indistinguishable from offset-made paperbacks.

In the POD model, books are produced only after they have been ordered, so no copies are wasted. The Print on Demand option eliminates any overproduction, waste, and pollution generated by offset printing, and the need to store or recycle excess books. This makes it cost-effective and simple to produce small amounts of books (or even just one) at a time when small publishers find it difficult to justify the high costs of producing and storing a larger print run. It must be acknowledged that this isn't much different than direct sales that ship books to consumer's homes, and POD books are shipped in smaller quantities, therefore usually making more trips. For small presses, POD trades minimal startup costs for lower per-book profits since digitally printed books have a higher individual production cost than large print runs. Because POD technology is similar to digital printing, it currently has few "green" options like those discussed in Part II. However, the reduction of significant waste may make up for these drawbacks. But there is no one formula to publish each and every book sustainably. Each book project is different and requires a thorough examination of all issues of sustainability from publication to distribution for that particular title.

On a smaller scale there are options that publishers can consider when thinking about making the post-production phase of their books' lives more sustainable. Books are often packaged and shipped *aerobic disintegration* | A natural decomposition process that requires the presence of oxygen.

in basic cardboard boxes. Cardboard packaging is generally made from recycled paper fiber since its main purpose is to serve as a container and not decoration. Cardboard is also highly recyclable for these same reasons. One option for materials that are unsuited for recycling or reuse is to use fully compostable packaging. Because compost relies on **aerobic disintegration**, there would be fewer emissions related to the anaerobic decomposition that takes place in landfills. Compost also provides a nutrient-rich soil conditioner and natural pesticide that can be used in farms and gardens, providing future horticultural benefit for its user. However, compostable packaging might not be widely available, and many cities don't offer curbside composting bins, leaving it to the individual to compost at home. But as composting becomes more prevalent, publishers should be aware of it as an option for their compostable waste.

Another way to cut needless waste in distribution is for publishers to institute standards or incentives to prevent waste. Chelsea Green, a Vermont-based publisher, created the Green Partner Program in 2007. This program works directly with bookstores to reduce impacts by providing carbon-neutral shipping and by selling books on a nonreturnable basis. In return, Green Partners are featured in the publisher's newsletter and on their website. BookPeople (Austin, Texas), City Lights Bookstore (San Francisco, California), Tattered Cover (Denver, Colorado), and Powell's Books (Portland, Oregon) are just a few examples of independent bookstores that have joined Chelsea Green Publishing's Green Partner Program. Creating a community that works toward a common goal can increase awareness of the book industry's current environmental impact while simultaneously reducing it.

The distribution and retail branches of publishing are only one part of the system that gets a book from author to reader. But as all aspects of the publishing industry, it is deeply dependent upon the other parts, so it's difficult to prescribe change to one area without needing to revamp the entire system. For example, POD production (a possible solution for some) relies on having this traditional distribution system in place (which is part of the problem). There is a great need for industry collaboration and further expansion of options for publishers. Something that isn't often discussed is the inflexibility of the current system, which is what panarchy is all about: the more flexible and broad a system is, the easier it will be to

Chelsea Green Publishing

Since 1984, Chelsea Green Publishing has demonstrated its commitment to sustainable living in both content and practice. With a business model that seeks to integrate the triple bottom line theory, this independent publisher remains at the forefront of the industry by setting a powerful example with its sustainable publishing practices. Chelsea Green's compelling editorial mission not only offers ideas on how publishers can achieve a more environmentally, socially, culturally, and politically sustainable world, but then actualizes this vision through responsible printing practices and community partnerships. Chelsea Green, a founding member of the Green Press Initiative, uses recycled, chlorine-free paper on all of its books and catalogs, and utilizes soy-based inks when possible. The press runs its own distribution, has its own in-house sales team, and has also created a unique partnership with independent bookstores across the country, circumventing the need for remainder dealers. Moving away from the traditional book business paradigm, Chelsea Green Publishing's impressive model is mutually beneficial to both indie publishers and indie bookstores. It facilitates getting books into the hands of the customers without the unnecessary financial and environmental waste associated with conventional distribution and bookselling practices.

Resources:
www.chelseagreen.com/company
http://news.shelf-awareness.com/ar/theshelf/2010-04-23/chelsea_green_northshire_bookstore_in_new_partnership.html

adapt to disruptions in the system. The more options a publisher has on a book-to-book basis, the more adaptable they'll be able to make the business model for that title suitable for its market potential. This requires more options on the outside, but it also requires publishers to be flexible in their internal thinking. Not every book should have international distribution, but certainly some books tell stories that everyone should read. Not every book should be an e-book, but many scream for interactive content. These decisions happen within a publisher's acquisitions process, which will be discussed in Part III, but options affect outcomes, and publishers have to take all options into consideration.

Book production, like book distribution, leaves a lot to be desired in terms of sustainability, but also holds great potential for creative solutions. The next section will provide an in-depth exploration of out-of-house production and how traditional practices might viably be improved to accommodate more sustainable processes.

PART II: Out-of-House Production

biomass | Biological material from living or recently living organisms, specifically referring to trees removed from forests for paper production. When incinerated, biomass waste is capable of producing enough heat to be a potential alternative energy source.

The largest environmental impacts come from the physical production of a book. While this is typically outsourced to a printer, publishers make the ultimate choice in choosing printers, paper stock, and ink options. By familiarizing themselves with the impacts associated with physical book production and recognizing ways to reduce those impacts, a publisher can choose the most sustainable options for a given project. In this section, we will discuss how the decisions a publisher makes about a book's appearance affect the environment and ecosystems.

Paper

Deforestation

The largest environmental impact of standard publishing practices is the harvesting of **virgin fiber** for paper production. Virgin fiber is wood that is harvested specifically for paper manufacturing with no previous uses, and accounts for approximately two-thirds of the pulp entering American paper mills.[14] According to the United Nations Intergovernmental Panel on Climate Change, deforestation comprises 25% of all man-made carbon emissions, making tree harvesting a massive cause for concern.[15] As shown in Table 1 in Part I, deforestation accounts for 62.7% of all carbon emissions in the publishing industry. The vast majority of these emissions (61.22%) stem solely from the removal of **biomass** from forests while the required energy and resources for harvesting and transportation of wood fiber to paper mills account for the remainder (1.52%).[16] Harvesting trees *terrestrial biospheric carbon* | The carbon dioxide (CO_2) that is naturally stored by existing biomass.

old-growth forests | Sometimes referred to as intact or natural forests, old-growth forests have not been disturbed by deforestation. Trees in old-growth forests can range in age from 150–500 years.

plantations | A forest that has been replanted by logging companies after the removal of old-growth. Plantations usually consist of a single species, eliminating the original forest's biodiversity. Plantations also cannot repair interrupted terrestrial carbon sequestration or make up for emissions released by logging machinery.

for virgin fiber removes existing life-supporting resources that convert carbon in the atmosphere into oxygen in the air. Forests serve as an essential part of terrestrial carbon sequestration, storing 50% of terrestrial carbon stocks.[17]

While many perceive the term "deforestation" as the destruction of distant exotic rainforests, the rate at which trees are being harvested in close-to-home places is disconcerting. The Canadian Boreal Forest is one of the world's largest intact forests that spans from the country's westernmost border with Alaska all the way to the Atlantic Ocean, covering 53% of the country's terrain.[18] However, nearly 2.5 million acres are removed each year due to harvesting by the paper industry.[19] This is detrimental to the Canadian Boreal's ecosystem, which is home to endangered species such as the woodland caribou, wolverine, and Labrador marten.[20] The Canadian Boreal also stores 47.5 billion tons of terrestrial carbon, which is 7–11% of the world's total **terrestrial biospheric carbon**. This is equivalent to roughly seven times the amount of annual fossil fuel emissions around the world.[21]

Forests spanning the southeastern United States are also a common source of paper fiber. Home to more than 2,250 different plant species and 150 different species of trees, these forests are some of the most biologically diverse woodlands in North America.[22] Each year, more than five million acres are logged by the paper industry, 75% of which are **old-growth forests**. Often, these forests are clear cut and replaced with single-species pine **plantations**. If changes are not made to the current system, one in four acres of the natural forests in the southeastern United States will be replaced by plantations by 2040.[23]

While efforts to replace the loss of natural forests with plantations may appear to be a noble solution to an expanding problem, there are still significant environmental impacts to the initial loss of biomass. Pine plantations do not store carbon as efficiently as their hardwood or natural pine forest predecessors. The old-growth forests of the Canadian Boreal, which constitute nearly 80% of the country's logged forests, may not reach their pre-harvest levels of carbon storage for at least 200 years.[24] Researchers at The Ohio State University found that the carbon storage of regrown forests, even those that had been in recovery for seventy years, was approximately half the amount of nearby old-growth forests.[25] The soil stores the majority of the forest's terrestrial carbon stocks and its displacement during harvesting causes much of the disruption in carbon storage. The removal of trees not only contributes to greenhouse gas emissions by releasing the soil's stored carbon into the air but also leads to the desiccation of the soil and increased storm run-off into rivers and lakes.[26]

The loss of ecosystems also has social effects such as disrupting indigenous tribes' harvesting and hunting practices. The Canadian Boreal is home to approximately one million aboriginal peoples, all of whom are affected in numerous ways by the loss of natural forests,[27] including territorial issues like those of the Grassy Narrows First Nation of northern Ontario. The provincial government circumvented an established 1873 treaty to allow AbitibiBowater, a leading Canadian paper producer, to manage the Whiskey Jack and Trout Lake Forests. The tribe was then restricted from accessing certain areas, causing problems for nearly half of the tribe who still rely heavily on gathering local flora and hunting for subsistence and medicinal purposes. These violations of indigenous rights have resulted in a loss of nearly half of the biomass on the tribe's traditional land base. While companies like Abitibi have made efforts to replace lost trees, there are still negative effects that stem from plantations. Direct health implications affecting surrounding populations arise from the aerial spraying of fertilizers, herbicides, and pesticides, including headaches, rashes, nosebleeds, and SARD (severe airway restrictive disorder).[28] Though the tribe has received support chlorine| A toxic gas that causes respiratory irritation. At high inhalation rates, it can react with water-containing cells in the body to produce traces of hydrochloric acid.

resin| A sticky plant secretion commonly found in coniferous trees. Resins are removed from wood fiber during pulping processes. Resins can be used as bio-derived additives in inks and adhesives.

lignin| A naturally occurring chemical compound found in wood fiber. The presence of lignin in paper weakens it and causes it to yellow over time.

from organizations such as Amnesty International, they currently still struggle with regaining their territorial rights.[29]

Making Paper with Virgin Fiber

After trees have been harvested, they are debarked, chipped, and then pulped either chemically or mechanically. **Chemical pulping** (also known as kraft or sulfate processing) uses **sodium sulfide**, **sodium hydroxide**, and sometimes **chlorine** compounds to separate individual wood fibers from surrounding **resins** and **lignin**, preserving the full fiber length from the original source and making it an ideal pulping process for the production of fine papers.[30] The chemical pulping process is called "freesheet" or "woodfree," which refers to the absence of lignin in the finished product. The potentially misleading "woodfree" is being phased out as industry terminology, since the word implies that the product does not contain wood. Although chemical pulping requires less energy than mechanical pulping, it produces less usable material overall for papermaking. The bleaching process for chemically produced pulp aids in the delignification process and typically involves a combination of chlorination, alkaline extraction, and oxidation. The bleaching process makes a paper whiter, like most paper used in copiers and home printers.

Mechanical pulping, or "groundwood pulping," uses fewer chemicals and produces more pulp for each ton of wood, but consumes far more energy than chemical pulping. Wood is passed through a mill that grinds the logs into pulp, which produces bundles of fiber that typically include whole and broken fibers, lignin, and other wood resins. This pulp is typically weaker than that of chemical pulping since it does not preserve the full length of the wood fiber. Because of the lack of resin-stripping chemicals, the lignin that remains in the pulp decays over time and causes the produced paper to become brittle and discolor in sunlight, like the aged paperbacks you might find in a used bookstore. The wood residues that remain in the pulp also produce a product that is not as bright as that created by a chemical process. Mechanically produced pulp is typically bleached with milder compounds, such as hydrosulfites and peroxides, since chlorinated bleach would cause the lignin to become soluble. The resulting manufactured paper is typically used for newsprint or packaging.

Once the pulp has been produced, it is ready to be rolled into paper. If the paper mill has an integrated pulping process, then the pulp is kept in liquid form and transferred to the next stage of production. If pulping is done at a separate site, the pulp is dried into sheets, baled, and transported to the paper mill, which adds carbon emissions to the environment. The dried pulp must be converted back to a liquid form by a slusher—a circular metal tank where the pulp sheets are soaked and broken up by a series of blades. Once in liquid form, the pulp is refined to achieve desired paper qualities, such as those related to strength or porosity. These characteristics are determined by the speed at which the pulp passes through a bladed cone onto a mesh screen. Additives—such as clay, titanium dioxide, or calcium carbonate—can be incorporated into the mix either before or after the refining process to strengthen the paper and fill in microscopic gaps between fibers for smoothness. Rollers are used to squeeze some of the water out of the pulp through the mesh screen. The remaining water is removed as the paper mixture is transferred through a series of heated rollers. At this point, the paper can pass through additional sizing or coating stations. **Coated paper** is treated with substances such as chalk or china clay, while **uncoated paper** remains bare. Uncoated papers are suitable for basic text-based books, like novels, but may be susceptible to ink bleeds around images or other areas where ink is heavily laid on the page. Coated papers are typically used when details in the printing are *calendering*| A finishing process in which paper is passed through pressurized heated rollers to impose a certain finish to give it a smooth or textured feel.

important, as in art and photography books, since the coatings used help prevent bleeds by confining ink to specific parts of the page. These papers can be **calendered** to impose different finishes, such as rough or smooth.

Paper manufacturing is also an energy-intensive process. Traditionally, a paper mill's proximity to a body of water allowed it to draw power through hydroelectricity. More recently, increasing energy demands have caused a shift toward power sourced from the burning of coal and other nonrenewable resources like gas or oil. The production of one ton of paper can necessitate anywhere from three-quarters to two tons of oil equivalent.[31] Some mills recover and burn biomass waste left over from the pulping process for energy. While this can usually only generate half of the plant's total needs, it still serves to cut energy costs on behalf of the plant and makes use of something that would instead end up

Paper Weight

There are two different ways of discussing paper weight. In North America, it's described by the weight in pounds of a ream (or 500 sheets) of a specific sheet size. This number can correlate with the paper's thickness, but it may not always be the best method of determination as the weight will not be universal across all sheet sizes. For example, a 70 lb. stock on larger 25"×38" sheets would be thicker than a 50 lb. stock of the same size. However, that same 70 lb. stock would be thicker in a ream of smaller 23"×35" sheets of the same weight. Outside of North America, paper weight measurements are measured in grams per square meter (gsm). Because this measurement accounts for both the physical mass of a ream of paper and its dimensional size, it is universal and can be applied to any paper size. A paper stock that comes in larger 25"×38" sheets and weighs 100 gsm would be just as thick as smaller 23"×35" sheets of the same weight.

in a landfill.[32] Recovering in-house waste to power a plant is usually only feasible for those using chemical pulping since the process yields a higher amount of waste than mechanical pulping.

Making Paper from Recycled Fibers

Recycled paper goes through a similar papermaking process but uses wood fiber from existing paper in lieu of virgin fiber. The thought of recycled paper often conjures up an image of gritty, discolored text stocks of poor quality. While this may have been the case in the past, many paper manufacturers now offer recycled paper options that are as high in quality as papers made from 100% virgin fiber.

When choosing a recycled paper stock, it is important to note the difference between the recycled content and the **post-consumer waste** (PCW) content. Post-consumer waste is paper that has reached its

Recycled vs. Recyclable

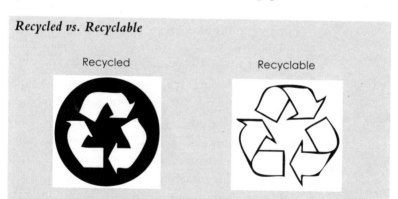

Recycled | Recyclable

Recycled...recyclable...same thing, right? Not exactly. Recycled means that the labeled product has been made from previously used or existing materials and uses little to no virgin materials for production. This is represented by the first image of the familiar arrows placed within a darkened circle. If there is a number inside the arrows, it represents the percentage of recycled materials that the product contains; the absence of a number indicates that the product comes from 100% recycled content. Recyclable, on the other hand, means that the product is capable of being recycled. This is indicated by a logo consisting of the same arrows, but without the outer circle. Numbers placed within this logo are generally reserved for plastics and indicate the resin ID code, which allows recycling facilities to sort compatible plastics for more efficient recycling.[3]

end user—the reader—and has since been reclaimed for recycling purposes. Paper stocks can be 100% recycled without containing 100% PCW content by using fiber sourced from **pre-consumer waste**, such as a printer's **make-ready**. The repurposing of post-consumer waste is a more sustainable option since there is no direct deforestation tied to its fiber sourcing. It also benefits the environment by removing the fiber from a landfill where it would continue to emit methane as it degrades. There is roughly five times the amount of post-consumer waste available for recycling as pre-consumer waste. Though post-consumer waste may be slightly more difficult to repulp due to the varied nature of contents that are sourced to recycling mills, the process has become more streamlined in recent years.

Choosing recycled paper over paper made from virgin fiber has many environmental benefits. The reduction of trees that would be harvested for virgin fiber prevents the loss of ecosystems, biodiversity, and a forest's storage potential for terrestrial biospheric carbon. The production of recycled paper requires less energy than the production of paper from virgin fiber and provides a significant reduction of hazardous emissions. Recycled paper mills reduce total energy consumption by 44%, net greenhouse gas emissions by 38%, **particulate matter** emissions by 41%, wastewater by 50%, solid waste by 49%, and wood use by 100%.[34] Unfortunately, high-quality paper recycled from post-consumer waste is typically more expensive than its virgin fiber counterpart, but not detrimentally so. Publishers may also encounter difficulty finding a recycled stock that has the weight or color specifications they need for a specific project. This is because printers must purchase paper in large quantities and will only offer paper stocks that their clients will use. Consumer demand plays a large part in the availability of high-grade recycled paper stocks, and as more publishers opt for more sustainable paper options, hopefully paper manufacturers will offer more stock options.

To manufacture recycled paper, the sourced waste must be repulped, cleaned of debris, **de-inked**, and often bleached. Sourcing pulp from recycled content is significantly more efficient than either the chemical or mechanical pulping process used for virgin fiber, as illustrated in Table 2.

Table 2. Required Bulk Material to Produce One Ton of Usable Pulp for Paper Production[35]

Pulping Process	Kraft (Chemical) Pulping	Mechanical Pulping	Pulping from Recycled Materials
Required Amount	4.4 tons	2.2 tons	1.4 tons
Efficiency Rate	23%	45%	71%

Recycled paper mills have a more efficient pulping process because the fibers have already been extracted from the virgin source during its initial pulping process, requiring less energy to produce the same amount of fiber.

The reclaimed pulp is processed to remove any ink, adhesives, coatings, staples, or other contaminants. These processes use chemical **surfactants**, resulting in a sludge-like waste. Sometimes, this sludge is repurposed as fertilizer, but this can be hazardous since some of the inks that have been removed from the pulp may contain toxic heavy metals. The sludge can also be reintegrated into the mill by using **recovery boilers** to produce an alternative source of energy. Otherwise, this sludge exits the mill as waste.

While recycled content often requires bleaching to achieve the level of whiteness desired in fine paper stocks, it requires less chemical processing than its virgin-sourced counterpart since the majority of recovered paper fibers have been previously bleached during their first production cycle. Many recycled paper mills use hydrogen peroxide or oxygen bleaching methods to prevent the harmful effects of chlorine in the mill's **effluent**. When chlorine is present with wood and water in a paper mill, it can produce **dioxins** that are released with a mill's wastewater. Certifications of varying levels exist to ensure that a paper has been processed without the use of chlorine. **Totally chlorine-free** (TCF) paper has been manufactured with absolutely no chlorine. However, this can currently only be applied to paper made from 100% virgin fiber since chlorine may have been used in the initial processing of paper made from recycled content. The **processed chlorine-free** (PCF) certification can be applied to recycled papers and ensures that no chlorine was used in its most recent production cycle. PCF certification also mandates that the paper has a minimum of 30% PCW content. **Elemental chlorine-free** (ECF) paper is processed using chlorine dioxide instead of elemental chlorine. This reduces the formation of chlorinated organic compounds, like dioxins, but chlorine dioxide can still be a problematic component released in the mill's effluent.

One potential issue involving recycled paper production is the life cycle of the fiber itself. Due to the necessary processing methods of recycling, fibers are weakened and shortened each time they are repulped. Fiber can only be recycled four to six times before it begins to break down too much to be turned into a viable paper option. By adding a percentage of virgin fiber, reprocessed pulp can increase in terms of strength and whiteness. This is one reason why there are many recycled paper options not made from 100% recycled content. Adding virgin fiber to recycled content helps extend the overall life cycle of the fiber and minimizes landfill contributions.

Exploring Alternative Fiber Options

In addition to recycled paper, many **alternative fibers** are becoming more prevalent as the demand for more sustainable paper options increases. In fact, until the 1800s, paper was typically made from non-wood sources like cotton. But over the past two centuries, European and North American countries have shifted toward wood-based paper products due to increasing paper demand and the abundance and proximity of wood fiber as a papermaking resource. In comparison, **tree-free** pulp makes up nearly half of paper production in countries like China and India, which have fewer hardwood forests and more viable alternative crop sources. Asia produces nearly 86% of the world's non-wood pulp for paper production, while Europe and North America combined produce only 4%.[36]

The range of tree-free paper options encompasses a vast number of organic and synthetic materials. Bamboo can re-grow from roots without being replanted, minimizing topsoil loss. Bamboo plants also reach maturity significantly quicker than trees and can grow more than fifty feet high in the span of four years. However, these plants are typically sourced from Asia, and the emissions and impacts related to shipping can potentially outweigh the pulp's benefits as an alternative to wood in North America.

Hemp is another option. Its fibers are strong and durable and require minimal bleaching due to their naturally light coloration. However, the cultivation of hemp is illegal in many countries, including the

tree-free | A designation for paper made from alternative fibers, often grown agriculturally, such as hemp, cotton, or kenaf.

United States. The processed fiber can be imported from other countries where cultivation is legal, such as Canada and China, but may result in additional transportation-related impacts.

Kenaf is grown in the southern United States and produces six to ten tons of fiber per acre each year. Closely related to okra and cotton crops, kenaf can be cultivated to create twine or cloth. Kenaf can be grown specifically for harvesting fiber and not for flowers or fruit so there is less need for chemical pesticides. Like hemp, it is a naturally light-colored fiber that requires minimal bleaching in paper production.

Cotton fiber is often used for the production of fine premium papers. The cotton plant provides durable fibers that require little bleaching and contain no lignin, which dismisses the necessity of chemical softeners. However, cotton cultivation requires more water than any of the other non-wood paper options. Cotton also currently exists as a significant international commodity and steering its cultivation towards paper production could have negative economical and social implications, especially in developing countries.

Agricultural residues, also called agri-fiber or agri-pulp, are made from various parts of wheat, rice, sugarcane bagasse, flax, and other crops that are not used for food or other primary harvesting purposes. These fibers are typically treated as a waste product. In North America alone, farmers burn approximately 262 million tons of agricultural residues each year simply to dispose of them. This not only increases air pollution by releasing emissions and particulates into the air, but could also be a missed opportunity for additional income for farmers.[37] The harvesting of these fibers requires no additional dedicated land, meaning it would not deprive necessary natural resources for production. However, there is a lack of proper processing plants for agri-pulp and adaptation on a large scale would be necessary to make processing it a viable option.

In addition to organic fibers, many synthetic sources are available for non-wood, paper-like alternatives. Melcher Media has produced a line of books using polymeric paper called DuraBooks, including William McDonough and Michael Braungart's *Cradle to Cradle:*

Remaking the Way We Make Things. The "paper" used in these books comes in a variety of weights, takes four-color ink processes, and uses no wood fiber in production. The paper is made from plastic resins and inorganic fillers that have the potential for **upcycling**. However, recycling these synthetic papers requires special facilities that are not widely available and the books can often end up in landfills. Plastic polymer "paper" is usually derived from petroleum and may require specially formulated inks, primers, and spray powder treatments to reduce static while on a printing press.

Mineral-based paper alternatives use little to no water in their production processes, release fewer emissions, and use just under half the energy of typical paper production. Many of these options are naturally bright depending on the minerals used, and may require little to no bleaching. They are durable, water resistant, and considered highly recyclable. But since recycling facilities are not widely available for these materials, books made from mineral alternatives have a high risk of ending up in landfills. Also, the range of printing options is limited as they are not highly receptive to ink jet or laser printing processes. The necessary binding materials for sheets of mineral-based paper may also contain petroleum-based plastics, compounding the end product's toxicity.

Difficulties arise in increasing the market share of non-wood fibers due to a lack of facilities for the production of tree-free papers. Some fibers require specialized presses depending on the paper's surface qualities. Shifting to tree-free fibers is not a perfect solution to the environmental impacts of paper production, but can be explored as a potential

upcycling| Closely related to the cradle to cradle theory, this is the idea of recycling a product into one that is longer lasting or more usable than it was originally. This is opposed to downcycling, in which the new product is degraded in order to be reused.

way to reduce the rate of hardwood deforestation. Additionally, nearly all tree-free papers lack environmental certifications that would assure sustainable sourcing and production methods. With significant consumer demand by publishers and consumers alike, these alternative fiber options may become more accessible alternatives in the future.

Paper Certifications

Paper certifications can be used to verify that a paper's fiber was harvested using environmentally, economically, and socially sustainable methods. A variety of labels are used, including self-declared labels like "Printed on 100% PCW Paper," but this section will focus on third-party labels. Often, certifications are leveraged by third-party organizations, which are usually non-profit in order to prevent problematic conflicts of interest or potential **greenwashing** by the product's manufacturer. The responsible use of credible **ecolabels** allows certified companies to communicate valuable information to their customers. The companies are able to point to specific ways in which they have demonstrated their commitment to sustainable practices with transparency, while proving they have successfully met rigorous requirements by measuring up to the public scrutiny of the certification program.

Forest Stewardship Council™

The Forest Stewardship Council (FSC), established in 1993, is an international non-profit organization that currently provides the most respected certification in the publishing industry and is supported by the World Wildlife Federation International and Greenpeace. The FSC provides forest management

(FM) certifications, which ensure that harvesting takes place under socially and environmentally responsible conditions, as well as **chain of custody** (COC) certifications, which traces the paper product through all stages of production—from harvesting and pulping through to distribution. Such certifications can be obtained through accredited bodies that verify that the company's business practices align with the ten core principles of the FSC, shown here in Table 3.

Table 3. The Ten Core Principles of the FSC[38]

1. Compliance with all applicable laws and international treaties
2. Demonstrated and uncontested, clearly defined, long-term land tenure and use rights
3. Recognition and respect of the rights of indigenous peoples
4. Maintenance or enhancement of long-term social and economic well-being of forest workers and local communities and respect of worker's rights in compliance with International Labour Organisation (ILO) conventions
5. Equitable use and sharing of benefits derived from the forest
6. Reduction of environmental impact of logging activities and maintenance of the ecological functions and integrity of the forest
7. Appropriate and continuously updated management plan
8. Appropriate monitoring to assess the condition of the forest, management activities and their social and environmental impacts
9. Maintenance of High Conservation Value Forests (HCVFs) defined as environmental and social values that are considered to be of outstanding significance or critical importance
10. In addition to compliance with all of the above, plantations must contribute to reduce the pressures on and promote the restoration and conservation of natural forests

Additionally, the FSC has a controlled wood certification that displays the percentage of non-certified material within a certified-product, ensuring that the wood fiber was sourced without illegal harvesting methods or violating the civil rights of workers and indigenous peoples. The FSC does not condone the presence of **genetically modified organisms** (GMOs) and monitors forests classified as **High Conservation Value Forests** (HCVFs), which can contain significant ecological values such as high biodiversity, endangered ecosystems, or the social values that are critical to a community's livelihood or their spiritual or cultural identity.

The FSC provides three different labeling categories:

- The FSC Pure label ensures that all fiber contained in the product is sourced from FSC-certified forests.
- The FSC Mixed Sources label allows for a mixture of fiber from certified forests, controlled wood sources, recycled wood, or recycled fiber.
- The FSC Recycled label ensures that the product contains 100% PCW content.

The Sustainable Forestry Initiative

The Sustainable Forestry Initiative (SFI) is currently one of the fastest growing sustainable certification programs. SFI certification is only available for forests in North America, as the program's standards were developed specifically with these forests in mind. The governing board of the SFI is divided into equal sections that represent economic, social, and environmental sectors. Like the FSC, the SFI provides certifications for forest management, chain of custody, and fiber sourcing. However, the SFI was launched by the American Forest and Paper Association, a coalition of forestry industry associations that represents 90% of industrial forestland in the United States. This causes concern that their interests may lie with the economic prosperity of the industry and not with the promotion of sustainable forestry practices. In fact, in 2009 ForestEthics—a North American nonprofit environmental organization—filed complaints with the U.S. Federal Trade Commission and Internal Revenue Service citing that the SFI was using false labels to drive sales of their products.[39]

The SFI's labeling system also has some flaws. One example is a company's ability to choose either a percentage credit or a volume credit when obtaining COC certification. For example, if a paper manufacturer uses 50% SFI-certified content for a specific paper stock, they can either label the product 50% certified, or they can label *half* the product 100% certified. The misrepresentation of a product's ecological qualities is a disingenuous practice that can lead to confusion among consumers.

The Programme for the Endorsement of Forest Certification

The Programme for the Endorsement of Forest Certification (PEFC) is an international non-profit founded in 1999 and based in Geneva, Switzerland. Despite its independent status as a non-governmental organization (NGO), PEFC bases its Sustainable Benchmark criteria on existing governmental standards set by the Ministerial Conference on the Protection of Forests in Europe, the African Timber Organization, and the International Tropical Timber Organization. Like the FSC and SFI, the PEFC provides certifications for forest management and chain of custody. However, usage of the PEFC logo is more relaxed than the standards for usage of the FSC logo. The PEFC requires only 70% of paper fiber content to come from PEFC-certified forests. This means that 30% of the fiber content can come from uncontrolled sources that may be executing unsustainable practices.

Other Certifications

In addition to the criteria set by these direct certification programs, paper products can use logos indicative of additional standards. Canopy (formerly Markets Initiative) is a non-profit organization that advocates the adoption of sustainable practices by publishers and paper producers and provides an Ancient Forest Friendly (AFF) certification for paper products. This certification requires that all the fiber used in the product have ecological attributes, using any mixture of pre- or post-consumer waste, agricultural residues, or FSC-certified virgin fiber. The AFF certification also mandates that all products must have PCF or TCF certification. The Rainforest Alliance (RA) is an FSC accreditation body that allows for the use of their logo if a product has gained FSC certification through their SmartWood program. The RA also provides a separate sustainable agriculture certification and advocates sustainable tourism and environmental education programs.

The Book Industry Environmental Council (BIEC) has proposed a certification program and a corresponding ecolabel that specifically tracks the sustainable choices of book publishers. Publishers earn points based on their efforts in the following five categories: Content of Book Paper, Reducing Paper Consumption and Waste, Minimizing Climate Impact, Toxics and Pollution Prevention, and Corporate Policies and Goals. To obtain "Top Tier" certification, a publisher must earn 600 total points for a given title. The BIEC Middle Tier and Lower Tier require 500 and 400 points, respectively. The goal of a structured point system is to reduce the environmental impact of the publishing industry while drawing attention to the publisher's accountability in the process.

Emissions

Throughout the entirety of a book's production process, many toxic substances are discharged through gas, liquid, and solid waste emissions. In fact, the pulp and paper industry emit almost 10% of all manufacturing carbon dioxide emissions in the United States. Power plant boilers release **sulfur dioxide** and **nitrogen dioxide** into the atmosphere through fuel combustion. These gases can cause haze and acid rain, damaging bodies of water, forests, and buildings and causing poor air quality and respiratory problems. The pulp and paper industry ranks fourth in both **volatile organic compound** (VOC) emissions, which combine with nitrogen dioxide to produce **ozone**, as well as in emissions of particulate matter released through fuel combustion and the papermaking process, which can cause respiratory and cardiovascular problems upon human exposure. The pulp and paper industry ranks fifth in the United States for emissions of **hazardous air pollutants** (HAPs), which are known to cause cancer and birth defects. Sulfur dioxide emissions emit the rotten egg-like odor commonly associated with kraft mills and can lead to respiratory problems. Mercury is released through both fuel combustion and the use of caustic soda in kraft processing (though more modern mills have adapted mercury-free processes). Mercury can cause damage to the kidneys, nervous system, and gastrointestinal tract.[40]

The processes for making paper require a great deal of water, a percentage of which exits the mills as a **by-product** that carries harmful substances. Paper mills that produce bleached, chemically processed pulp made from virgin fiber use between 4,000 and 12,000 gallons of water for every ton of fiber produced.[41] The wastewater leaving the mills often contains dioxins, which are known carcinogens, and dioxin-like compounds such as **furans**. The release of nitrogen and phosphorous compounds in effluent leads to the growth of toxic algae in the body of water in which it is deposited, killing inhabiting fish and other organisms. Paper mill

ozone|In the Earth's upper atmosphere, ozone filters harmful UV light and prevents it from reaching the planet's surface. However, when it remains close to the surface, it is a pollutant that can cause lung irritation and respiratory problems in humans and can damage certain plants.

hazardous air pollutants (HAPs)|This is a collective name for air pollutants named and regulated under Section 112 of the Clean Air Act. These pollutants are known environmental hazards.

furans|A type of dioxin. Observation shows that these chemical compounds are highly toxic and carcinogenic.

sulfur dioxide (SO_2)|A chemical compound that can cause environmental problems, such as acid rain, when present in emissions.

Joshua Martin

Joshua Martin assisted in the formation of the nonprofit Environmental Paper Network (EPN), a coalition working to advance social and environmental responsibility in the pulp and paper industry. As the director, Martin has been instrumental in effecting significant improvements in an attempt to reform the industry. His commitment to improving industry standards is reflected in his contributions to increase education and his commitment to shift market demand to more sustainable paper options. EPN's project What's In Your Paper (whatsinyourpaper.com) provides educational tools to increase public awareness of responsible paper options and encourage informed paper purchasing policies. Martin's activism helped move organizations like Office Depot, Victoria's Secret, Random House, and the U.S. House of Representatives toward dramatically shifting their paper choices, which helps drive an expanding market for environmentally responsible paper.

Resources:
www.environmentalpaper.org
www.whatsinyourpaper.com
www.thefreelibrary.com/
Joshua+Martin%3A+paper+pioneer-a0186319237

effluent also contains toxic substances that have been shown to negatively affect the endocrine and reproductive systems of various species of fish.[42]

Solid waste from paper production includes the portion of biomass waste that cannot be used for recovered energy, wastewater treatment sludge, lime sludge, and ash. Suspended solids released in effluent include lignin removed from wood fibers during the pulping process, toxic heavy metals, and organic compounds. These solids settle on the floor of the body of water, poisoning the food source for bottom-feeding organisms and blocking necessary nutrients from being released upwards into the water, subsequently creating a potentially permanent **abiotic environment**. Many toxic heavy metals are both fat-soluble and **biologically magnified**, meaning that their toxic effects increase as they are passed up through the food chain.[43]

When deposited into bodies of water, these solid emissions can affect the oxygen supply for nearby aquatic organisms. **Biochemical oxygen demand** (BOD) measures the amount of oxygen consumed by microorganisms and decomposing organisms that stem from these toxic emissions. Many mills attempt to reduce the emission of oxidizable compounds through effluent treatment plants. The efficiency of these treatments can be measured through surveying the **chemical oxygen demand** (COD) of these emissions.[44]

Solutions

Fortunately, treatment options are available for reducing the hazardous and climate-changing emissions of paper manufacturing. By employing the **closed-loop** theory of production, a paper mill or printer can function as a **totally effluent-free** (TEF) facility. Filtering and reusing wastewater not only prevents the release of toxic chemicals into local water sources, but also reduces the necessary intake of water for production purposes. Wastewater treatment involves the removal of suspended solids through physical screening methods and chemical treatments to reduce hazardous organic compounds in mill effluent.[45] The employment of chlorine-free processes prevents the toxic emission of chlorinated compounds into the surrounding bodies of water.

In kraft pulping facilities, sulfur dioxide emissions can be reduced through special hoods and venting equipment, a practice that has become more common since the passing of the **Clean Air Act**. Alkaline solutions applied to mill equipment condense the gases and funnel them into compounds to be incinerated in a limekiln or dedicated combustion unit. **Electrostatic precipitators** can be used to limit the release of particulate matter in air emissions.[46] By removing excess liquids from sludge and incinerating it in a recovery boiler, a mill can reduce its total solid waste sent to the landfill and have an additional energy source for the mill.

Because of the significant energy needs of each part of the publishing process, especially paper production, it is vital for companies to look for alternate power sources that do not deplete non-renewable resources such as coal and petroleum. Recovery boilers are certainly one part of the solution, as they power the plant while reducing net waste. Many other renewable energy options are also available, such as wind power, solar power, and hydroelectricity, which release no direct greenhouse gas emissions. Paper mills and printers should also be sure they are operating at maximum

Clean Air Act | A federal law enacted in 1963 (and expanded in 1970) by the United States Congress to control air pollution on a national level according to guidelines developed by the Environmental Protection Agency. Amendments in 1990 further addressed issues regarding pollution related to ozone depletion and acid rain.

electrostatic precipitators | These are devices that use the principles of magnetism to charge airborne particles and draw them out of the air.

biochemical oxygen demand (BOD) | A measurement of the effectiveness of water emission reduction programs. The figure is determined by measuring the amount of oxygen needed by aerobic biological organisms to break down any organic pollutants present in a water sample.

carbon offsets| A system by which an individual or an organization can compensate for their own carbon emissions by investing in energy alternatives, including wind power, hydroelectric energy, or other greenhouse gas reduction strategies.

offset lithography| A printing process in which images are offset onto another surface before being printed on a paper surface. Many larger printing projects are done by offset printing.

digital short-run printing| A printing system distinct from offset printing, digital presses print directly from a digital file and are most often used for smaller print jobs.

substrate| Any material that receives ink in the printing process. In book printing, the most common substrate is paper.

efficiency to ensure that power is not being wasted through unnecessarily draining production. Although the purchase of **carbon offsets** can "balance" any energy that is sourced from non-renewable resources, it is neither an ultimate nor a perfect solution.

Ink and Printing

Printing

Once paper has been manufactured, it is distributed to printers. When a book is ready to be printed, publishers send the main ingredients of a book—the manuscript and book cover, the paper specifications (text and cover stock choices), and shipping instructions—to the printer electronically. Print runs are typically produced through **offset lithography** or **digital short-run printing**.

Lithographic printing presses can either be sheet-fed or web-fed. Sheet-fed is a lot like it sounds: presses print on pre-cut press sheets of paper. Offset printing sheets are typically 28"×40", though this varies depending on the press's capabilities. Web-fed presses, on the other hand, draw paper off of large rolls. Due to the more consistent flow of paper, web-fed presses are typically used for very large print runs, including books, newspapers, and magazines. Just think of a scene from a movie where newspapers are being cranked out at high speeds, just before the headlines spin towards the screen. In both methods, the paper is folded and trimmed according to specifications after printing is complete.

Offset Lithography

Offset lithography is a planographic printing process in which the ink is laid flat onto the **substrate**, which is typically paper in book printing. This printing process relies on treating printing plates and substrates so that they are hydrophobic (water-resistant) on the areas that comprise the text and images to be printed and hydrophilic (water-absorbent) on the areas to be left blank. Printing plates are typically aluminum, paper, or plastic that function much like photographic negatives to accept and transfer images. The plate-wrapped cylinder accepts an oil-based ink and rejects water-based **fountain solutions** on the image area. As this cylinder rotates, it receives ink and water from two separate sets of rollers, and then transfers the ink-receptive images and text onto an offset cylinder. This cylinder is usually outfitted with a rubber blanket that transfers, or "offsets," the ink onto the substrate.

fountain solutions| A water-based solution used during offset lithographic printing to prevent non-image areas from accepting ink. These solutions are a large component of a printer's wastewater emissions.

Fountain solutions used in offset lithography are composed of water, nonvolatile chemicals such as hydrophilic gums and mineral salts, and volatile chemicals such as alcohol or alcohol substitutes. These solutions wet the substrate to prevent the ink laid onto the image area from bleeding onto the non-image area. Alcohol is a common component in these solutions to facilitate their evaporation after printing is complete. They can contain isopropyl alcohol, ethanol, or substitutes such as glycol ethers or ethylene glycol—all of which release VOCs into the air as they evaporate. Before the 1980s, the concentration of alcohol in fountain solutions was as high as 35% but has since declined to approximately 5%–10%.[47]

During the printing process, fountain solutions flow constantly to keep the substrate wet. To calibrate the presses and get the mixture of fountain solutions and ink right, presses must run at real speeds even before the print run starts. This creates test printing materials that are waste, referred to as make-ready, or "broke," and necessitates as much as an additional 10% of the total materials necessary for the print run itself. Make-ready is typically recycled as pre-consumer waste.

Since blankets, rollers, and other components are reused, they need to be washed when changing inks or ink colors. This may be after each single-color ink run or after the print run is complete. The cleaning solutions used to wash this equipment are composed of petroleum-based solvents, detergents, and water. Although they remove ink quickly from printing components, they often contain more than 60% VOCs.[48] Presses typically use one-third the amount of press cleaners in relation to fountain solutions. Both substances contaminate effluent and surrounding air.

Digital Printing

Digital printing uses either a **toner** or **inkjet** system. For presses using toner, the dry pigments adhere to the substrate using heat. This process uses no alcohol, so it emits no VOCs, but can cause respiratory problems and irritate existing respiratory conditions, such as asthma and bronchitis.[49] The powder used in digital printer toner is petroleum-based and cannot be recycled. Inkjet printing sprays water and solvent-based ink directly onto paper, which can include alcohols that contribute to VOC emissions. Publishers may be limited by the fact that digital presses do not always produce the high quality results achieved with offset printing. These presses also offer a limited number of ink and paper options and may encounter difficulty printing on recycled paper and alternative fibers.

In spite of these limitations, digital presses do have environmental benefits. By not requiring the large amount of make-ready necessary for ink calibration or fountain and cleaning solutions as offset presses do, they produce fewer VOC emissions and toxic effluent. Take the Hewlett-Packard Indigo digital press—its inks release no hazardous air pollutants or particulate matter, but still release VOCs due to their petroleum base.[50] In 2007, the HP Indigo 5500 was released with an on-press oil recycling system that separates water from the condensed oil that is produced by the inks and reduces consumption and waste by 50%.[51] HP has also implemented successful initiatives for recycling used hardware and print cartridges and reducing energy consumption and emissions.[52]

When choosing between offset and digital printing, publishers examine the costs and benefits of each, notably when it comes to print volume. While offset printing offers more eco-friendly choices like vegetable-based inks and a wider variety of paper options, it is typically only cost effective for book runs of over 2,000 copies. If a publisher estimates that only 1,000 copies of a book will sell, it is usually best to choose to print the book on a digital press. If an overprinted title ends up in a landfill or recycling center without reaching an end user, there's little reason to celebrate the alternative ink options and reduced VOC emissions in its production.

Waterless Offset Printing

If an offset print run is suitable for the project, publishers could consider the use of **waterless offset printing**. Waterless printing uses specialized silicone plates that transfer ink directly onto the substrate without the need of fountain solutions, which vastly decreases VOCs and wastewater emissions. The non-use of fountain solutions also means less make-ready waste due to a reduced need for ink calibration. Printers who choose to implement waterless technology can produce highly efficient print runs that are the same quality as regular lithography. However, some roadblocks prevent this process from being widely available. The necessary silicone plates are more expensive than typical offset printing plates. Press operators must also be trained to maintain a specific temperature balance in order for ink to transfer properly without becoming too runny or dry. While only a limited number of printers use this process in North America, it is widely available in Japan and other countries that have laws and incentives for reducing VOC emissions.

water-miscible| A
substance that is able
to mix with water
in any proportion to
form a completely
homogenous, or
uniform, solution.

Sustainable Printing Options

If waterless printing is not a feasible option for a
book's print run, standard lithographic offset printing has options for reducing VOC emissions. Printers
can choose fountain solutions that are structurally
similar to typical solutions, but use glycol ethers as
a less volatile substitute for alcohol. The solution's
additives are diluted in water in small quantities
(typically 2–4 ounces per gallon of water) and can
produce a final fountain solution with less than 3%
VOCs by weight.[53]

Sustainable options are available for reducing
labor, waste, and emissions associated with cleaning
solutions in typical lithography. Cleaners containing
water-miscible solvents can be diluted with water
instead of harsher chemical solvents. Many vegetable oil-based blanket washes require no special
storage, help to condition printing blankets, and can
contain VOC content as low as 5%. Another cleaning
option is terpene cleaners derived from citrus and
wood products. These are typically more expensive
than average cleaners, but produce minimal VOC
emissions.[54]

In addition to alternative cleaning solution
options, a printer can also opt to change its practices
to be more conducive to natural cleaning. Most traditional ink systems are petroleum-based. By using
a water-washable ink system, a printer can eliminate
the need for harsh cleaners that contain solvents that
release VOCs. A printer may also consider installing
automatic blanket washers. By having automated
equipment that cleans press blankets with sprays or
brushes, printers can reduce the need not just for
VOC-containing solvents, but also worker contact
with potentially hazardous solvents.

Hemlock Printers

Hemlock is an important leader in promoting environmental awareness and sustainability. An emphasis on environmental stewardship is evident in every aspect of their business practices and operations, not just in what they produce. Focusing on efficiency, recycling, smart purchasing, and developing methods that minimize the use of harmful compounds, the Vancouver, BC-based printer is a two-time winner of the Print Action Environmental Printing Award. They have been named Canada's most environmentally progressive printer for the past five consecutive years. In 2008, they won the Heidelberg Eco Printing Award for "Most Sustainable Printing Company."

As the first FSC-certified chain-of-custody printer in the Pacific Northwest, as well as the first printer in North America to commit to an Ancient Forest Friendly policy, Hemlock prints at least 40% of its jobs on paper containing at least 10% post-consumer recycled content. They provide eco-audits for all of their jobs and offer eco-alternatives on all print bids to raise awareness among customers who might have assumed that traditional paper and print choices are the only affordable options. Hemlock uses offset presses for larger jobs and very resource-efficient HP Indigo digital presses for shorter runs. With offset jobs, the company created the award-winning program called Off Cuts for Charity, which provides printing services to qualified charitable organizations by offering otherwise-empty space on existing print runs, thus utilizing the entire press sheet.

In their low-odor pressroom, all printing is alcohol-free. Blanket washes mix with water and evaporate so slowly that volatile emissions are at a minimum. Process waters are reused multiple times before on-press evaporation or in-developer treatment. Waste solvents and old rags are used as a clean-burning fuel; the ash is later used for cement making. Hemlock uses inks low in VOCs, offers vegetable based inks, and calculates the amount of ink needed for each job before it begins to reduce waste. Any leftover ink is mixed to make custom colors and stored for later use. Hemlock estimates that these measures save almost one metric ton of ink annually.

In 2004, Hemlock formed a Sustainability Committee. The committee consists of managers who identify ways to improve the print process and practicable ideas for increasing sustainability and environmental awareness company-wide. One such idea was to set up a collection point for used electronic appliances and equipment for repair or recycling. This easy diversion of e-waste has kept over 2,000 pounds of techno-trash out of landfills.

In the office, Hemlock uses only 100% PCW office paper and offers only organic, fair trade coffee. Light sensors adjust output to reduce power consumption. Half of Hemlock's fleet is run on biodiesel (carbon offsets are purchased for the rest), and they recycle all paper, metals, wood palettes, compostable materials, batteries, light bulbs, electronics, wastewater, and over 90% of all hard and soft plastics. Hemlock even rearranges carpet tiles in the office until they are all evenly worn before sending them back to the manufacturer for recycling.

Resources:
www.hemlock.com

When selecting a printer for a sustainably produced project, it is helpful to examine its environmental policies and goals. If you are a publisher looking to increase your company's sustainability commitment, seek printers that are FSC-certified to ensure that a company's environmental initiatives are legitimate and not merely an act of greenwashing. Printers with sustainability initiatives are more likely to offer eco-friendly options and are usually more willing to work with publishers to help achieve a specific product's environmental goals. By establishing a good channel of communication with a printer, publishers are also able to attain concrete information on the potential impacts of products and practices employed during printing.

Ink

The printing industry goes through approximately two billion pounds of ink each year.[55] Offset inks are made up of pigments or dyes, binders, and vehicles. Ink gets its coloration from either powdered pigments or liquid dyes. Pigments lie on the surface of the substrate while dye-based inks tend to soak into the paper, which can lead to uncontrolled **bleeds** and lesser quality image reproduction on porous surfaces like uncoated paper. Dye-based inks can be difficult to remove in recycling depending on the level of saturation in the substrate. Resins and other liquids form the vehicles that make the ink fluid and allow the pigment or dye to be imposed on the substrate. Inks can contain additives to modify the ink for optimum press performance, including defoamers and wax. Most additives and vehicles in offset inks are petroleum-based.[56]

After the ink has been laid onto the page, it must be dried before the paper can be trimmed for binding. Often, inks are dried through **heatsetting**, which involves gas or electric drying ovens that dry off the solvents in the ink, leaving behind only the pigments or dyes. Not only does this add significantly to the energy requirements of a print run, but heat-set inks can also release 35%–45% of their VOC content into the air. Non-heatset drying processes, or "coldset," are better since they release only 2%–20% of the ink's VOC content.[57] And if the ink is heavily solvent-based, it can dry through a combination of evaporation into the air and penetration into the substrate. Some chemical curing methods also require the addition of certain catalysts to link and solidify the pigment molecules in order to facilitate fewer additional drying processes.

The ideal sustainable ink would be sourced from a renewable resource, produce minimal hazardous waste and emissions, and be easier to de-ink in the recycling process. While it might not be possible to always use ink with these qualities, many options produce the high-quality results of typical petroleum-based inks while reducing the associated VOC emissions.

Sustainable Ink Options

Inks that are formulated for **ultraviolet (UV) printing** are one potential option. These inks dry instantly upon UV exposure, eliminating the need for heated dryers. This reduces the necessary solvent content in the ink, VOC emissions, and the energy usage associated with heatset drying processes. However, these ink-curing technologies come with a higher start-up cost for printers and the need for special training to properly operate equipment. Also, UV inks may potentially contain acrylate components, which can cause allergic reactions, irritation, and burns for press workers.

bleed| A printing term for ink that extends beyond the margins to the edge of the page.

black liquor| A byproduct of kraft pulping composed of lignin residues, hemicelluloses, and the inorganic chemicals used to extract individual paper fibers from the pulp mixture. Black liquor can be burned in recovery boilers as an alternative source of energy.

Vegetable-based inks are becoming increasingly available and can be used on regular offset presses without the need for additional equipment or training. Vegetable-based inks replace a percentage of the petroleum base with a bio-derived oil that can significantly reduce VOC emissions on-press. In the United States, soy-based inks are the most accessible option, while Canadian printers tend to use inks that contain canola or linseed oil. The American Soybean Association offers a Soyseal label for inks produced with certain percentages of soy oil in the ink's vehicle, which varies from 7%–40%. Inks can also be manufactured from distilled **tall oil**, gums, and wood resins from pine trees. Tall oil is a component of **black liquor**, a byproduct of the kraft pulping process—and provides an opportunity for paper and ink manufacturers to collaborate on more efficient recycling of waste products. However, vegetable-based inks do not dry as quickly as petroleum-based inks, which may lead to increases in time and resources that a printer might require or the need for prolonged heat-settings that increase energy consumption.

Currently, the ink production industry does not have the same level of environmental certification as the paper industry. Also, no chain-of-custody certifications or verifications are available to ensure the materials used were harvested sustainably. This means that inks made from vegetable oils may be derived from genetically modified plants or come from farms with unsustainable harvesting and labor practices. If the plants are harvested from a source that is substantially distant from the ink manufacturer, emissions from transit will increase the ecological footprint of the product. However, the ink industry has made recent strides towards more environmentally aware practices. The National Association of Printing Ink Manufacturers has developed a Bio-derived Renewable Content (BRC) label to measure the content of natural renewable resources in inks. The label is accompanied by a BRC Index Number, which directly corresponds to the total percentage of bio-derived content of components such as pigments, oils, and waxes. The institution of a universal label for sustainably produced ink is an important step in providing transparency of the ink production process.

After the Paper and Ink

Coatings

Like all sustainable production decisions, the choice of book cover will have different effects on the quality of the product and its environmental ramifications. The shiny gloss or subtle matte of a book's cover comes from its coating. Two of the most common types of coatings are **varnishes** and **laminates**, both of which are also the most harmful. Varnishes are made up of many of the same petroleum-based substances found in inks and add to the VOC emissions of a print run. Many varnishes are clear, though pigment can be added to produce a tinted coating. If the inks used on the substrate are compatible, varnishes can be wet-trapped, or applied at the same time as the inks. Dry-trapped varnishes are applied as a separate process or pass through the printer after the ink has dried. Varnishes can make the substrate difficult to de-ink during recycling and add more contaminates to the sludge waste produced during the de-inking process. Laminates are applied either as a clear plastic film adhered to the substrate's surface or as a liquid spread over the substrate and cured like a varnish. While these coatings are typically composed of nylon, polyester, or polypropylene to increase durability, all are completely non-recyclable.

Protective coatings for book covers reduce potential damage to books while traveling long distances between printer, publisher, distributor, bookstore, and consumer. And while eco-friendly alternatives to non-recyclable petroleum-based coatings do exist, they may not always offer the same level of durability as laminates. Publishers more often than not choose to varnish or laminate their books because unprotected books will eventually show signs of damage and be deemed hurt, or unsellable, and will then never reach the end user. But publishers can choose laminates more responsibly by thinking ahead and determining a title's expected lifecycle. A publisher might decide an aqueous or UV coating may be adequate protection for book covers, eliminating the need to use petroleum-based components.

Aqueous coatings are applied in-line on press after ink has dried. These coatings come in gloss, dull, and satin finishes and are non-flammable, glueable, and resistant to yellowing. They are typically composed of polymeric resin, wax, silicone for rub resistance or slipperiness, surfactants for improved leveling during application, and additives such as defoamers or brighteners. The coating dries by removal of water and ammonia from coating solids through evaporation and absorption. The absence of a heatset drying method saves both energy usage and release of emissions. VOC emissions are further reduced since aqueous coatings are water-based instead of oil-based.

UV coatings are also applied in-line on press. They are available in glossy or matte finishes and are more protective than varnish or aqueous coatings. These coatings are instantly cured with UV exposure, which reduces production time for increased press efficiency. Because of the hardness of these coatings, they may be potentially difficult to de-ink during the recycling process. However, they are better at preserving color and graphics and are more protective than aqueous coatings, making them a viable substitution when the durability of a laminate is required.

Binding
The next step in the process is binding everything together into a book to be shipped to distributors and publisher. Many printers do this job in an on-site bindery, but printers who lack a bindery of their own will use further transit to ship the materials to another

site. A number of different binding options exist, but the most common technique for trade paperbacks is **perfect binding**. Perfect binding entails folded and gathered (F&G) **signatures** glued together at the spine to the cover of the book. The adhesive used is a hot-glue melt made up of petroleum-based polymers, waxes (either animal, plant, or petroleum based), and/or resins (plant based) applied at room temperature and then heated to adhere to the paper, solidifying as it cools. During the heating process, VOCs in the hot glue are released. The hot glue can also create obstacles in the recycling process: not only will the heat involved release more VOCs, but also—and more technically problematic—the glue becomes sticky again and can stick to the machinery and adhere to the fibers in the pulp mash.

The ideal solution for bookbinding would release few emissions during application, be easy to remove for recycling, and provide durable support for keeping the components of the book together. However, the three main types of hot-melt glues don't quite meet this goal. Polyvinyl acetate (PVA) adhesives can be applied at room temperature and set into a flexible emulsion. They are nontoxic and release no VOCs or HAPs, but are made from petroleum-based substances. While viable recycling options exist for this type of adhesive, it is not as strong as other options and sets more slowly, causing issues in production and overall durability. Polyurethane (PUR) adhesives are a slightly better option even though they are also hot glue melts, but since they are not water-soluble they can be filtered out during the recycling process. Ethylene vinyl acetate (EVA) adhesives are similar to those found in hot glue guns and soften when reheated, which can make them difficult to recycle.[58]

signature| A section of book pages gathered together after folding and cutting; multiple signatures are then gathered together and bound. Common page counts in one signature are sixteen or thirty-two.

If a publisher determines that perfect binding is the best option, they should explore the use of cool-melt adhesives as they release fewer VOCs than typical hot-melt glues.

Mechanical binding methods, such as saddle stitching, post binding, or spiral binding, lack VOC-releasing adhesives and are easier to remove during recycling. They may be an appropriate option for durability depending on the title (such as a cookbook or technical manual), but may not provide the permanent structure of an adhesive-based method like perfect binding.

Though some of these individual solutions may seem too small to matter, they can make a big difference when used together. As previously mentioned, paper production and printing makes up for the largest percentage of emissions by the publishing industry. If employed on a significant scale, these more sustainable options could help the industry reduce its carbon footprint in the years to come. While the availability of many of these options may seem out of a publisher's hands, it's important to remember that significant demand will drive paper producers and printers to offer these services and products to their clientele. The next section will explore in-house production and how publishers can implement sustainable solutions fully throughout the operations of their press.

Acquisitions & Editing

Truly responsible publishing starts with book acquisition. We've all heard the pejorative "What a waste of a tree!" describing works that don't measure up to someone's personal opinion of a good book. Acquisitions editors, who decide which manuscripts to publish, do have to take this clichéd insult into consideration by weighing a book's potential social or cultural value against the methods used to make it. To do this, acquisitions editors need to ask questions that go beyond the basic "Will this book sell?" when reviewing a manuscript for publication. It is important for everyone interested in sustainable publishing to understand what "cost" and "value" mean in the context of the triple bottom line, which is concerned with measuring the social and environmental impacts of an activity as well as economic performance. Even if a clever guide to the latest reality show will likely prove to be successful in terms of sales, is its contribution to society worth the resources that will be used in its production? Acquiring editors might begin asking: What is the societal value of the potential book? Is it worth the environmental and social costs?

The acquisitions editor functions as a gatekeeper between the worlds of unpublished manuscripts and published books. A sustainably minded acquisitions editor will be conscious of the gravity of the decision to bring a manuscript to the printed page with regard to the long-term social and environmental consequences as well as short-term financial gains. Beyond the larger picture of what to publish, publishers, acquisitions editors, and authors can be aware of smaller—but nevertheless, important—steps towards greener practices. Accepting only electronic query letters, submissions, and manuscripts is one policy that can reduce unnecessary paper waste. If authors choose to print material, publishers might encourage them to keep it single-spaced and to print on the front and back of paper (as submission guidelines permit). Rejected hardcopy manuscripts should ideally be recycled, but recycling should be thought of as a second-best alternative to reducing the use of paper materials in the first place.

Many unsolicited submissions don't fall within the scope of what is ultimately accepted or even seriously considered for publication by the publisher for print. The **slush pile**—notably named after the very waste that comes from the paper factory—is publishing jargon for unsolicited manuscripts sent to publishers by authors and literary agents. If publishing houses maintain up-to-date and highly visible submissions guidelines and a backlist that showcases preferred genres, authors should be equally conscientious about where they send their manuscripts. This would keep young adult fiction writers from sending their manuscript to publishers of cookbooks. Authors don't always research thoroughly before submitting their work to publishers, but ensuring that this information is easily accessible will also conserve paper, ink, postage costs, and the acquiring editor's time.

While many editors have acquisitions as part of their job responsibilities, it is the sole responsibility for an acquisitions editor, often making them the first contact for an unpublished writer. Since most major publishers do not accept unsolicited manuscripts, those that do must cope with an onslaught of material. Authors can begin addressing their role in the sustainable publishing industry by researching and targeting appropriate publishers; avoiding the use of services that blanket query publishers; and writing professional, effective query letters and proposals to decrease the chance that they'll end up in the recycling bin. Above all, writers should thoroughly research the publisher they submit to, making sure to match their book with the publisher's submission guidelines.

As the industry moves toward an online and digital landscape, authors and publishers must stay as up-to-date and competitive as possible with changes in print media. Traditional practices, such as the printing and mailing of acceptance and rejection letters and editors working with hard copy, are increasingly falling by the wayside. A considerable amount of time, money, and waste can be saved by making all correspondence between editors and authors primarily electronic, and by employing digital tools like Microsoft Word's Track Changes or embedded indexing software to eliminate excess paper and shipping. However, while acquisitions editors may request that authors email their submissions as an attachment (in a Word document, for example), publishers might avoid this for a number of reasons. The document may be too large to send easily, the publishers might fear getting a computer virus, or authors may worry about the security of their manuscript. A primary hazard of distributing manuscripts via email is that privacy can be compromised through the inability to maintain control over viewing and distributing the electronic manuscript; luckily, there are some viable solutions for this, such as password protection, encryption, virus scans, and file sharing services.

Should a publisher wish to switch entirely to electronic acquisitions, an online submission manager program—although a fairly new technology with room for improvement—is a program that offers online submission forms for authors and an invaluable database for publishers that allows them to accept and manage digital submissions. Currently, a variety of submission managers exist at affordable prices, and most can be tweaked to fit the needs of any acquisition process unique to a press or publication. An excellent example of this online system is the submission manager offered by the Council of Literary Magazines and Presses (CLMP). It allows a publisher to accept submissions through its website, easily manage the genres that the press accepts, control the number of submissions an author can make, manage reading periods, track submissions automatically, maintain a complex database with information that is easily cross-referenced and searched, allow the publisher to control design features, send out automatic emails confirming that a submission has been received, accept or reject submissions individually or en masse, and create standard or personalized email rejections.

Many authors, editors, acquisitions editors, and indexers may prefer to primarily utilize hard copy manuscripts, and they should continue employing processes they've found works best for them. An indexer, for example, might prefer to mark a printed manuscript *trim size* | A book's final size after the excess edges have been removed and production is complete. Common trim sizes for trade books in the U.S. include 5.5"×8.5", 6"×9", 8.5"×11".

or use the manual 3"×5" index card method as she initially delineates entries and locators, but prints on both sides of the page, recycles the manuscript or index cards afterwards, and conducts the majority of her correspondences with the publisher via email to transmit files. Rethinking the publishing industry with sustainability in mind doesn't mean compromising the integrity of the finished product. Sustainable publishing simply means making responsible, informed decisions to reduce the environmental impact of the process to the extent that one is able to do so.

Design

Book designers are responsible for transforming a manuscript into a physical object. Book covers and interiors are created through the implementation of ideas and existing design standards that encompass the finished product's readability and overall aesthetic quality. Traditionally, production cost is the most limiting factor in determining everything from the number of colors used in printing to **trim sizes** and finalized page counts. While the design process has a significantly smaller impact than physical production, it is directly linked to the final printing decisions. If a book is designed without the consideration of a sustainable bottom line, there can be considerable waste produced during the book's print production process.

First and foremost, aesthetic does *not* need to be sacrificed for sustainability. To approach book design in a sustainable way, designers can commit to staying informed about the materials and processes a design requires. Technology evolves quickly and a more sustainable, more attractive option may have been developed since the last book you designed. Being involved in the design and sustainability community will make you a better designer. Adjust your design philosophy. Rather than considering only the needs of the author and the reader, take into consideration the larger picture: the immediate and long-term needs of the environment and society.

In the cradle to cradle (c2c) model of production, sustainability is incorporated into the design of the book itself. In this model, a product's ultimate destiny is considered and planned during its initial design; its recyclability or reusability is integrated from the start. In contrast, the more common cradle to grave model designs products with the assumption that they will eventually be thrown out or recycled. The c2c theory employs design and production techniques that maximize efficiency and minimize waste. For example, in considering a book's journey to a bookstore, designers should avoid elements that are highly susceptible to damage in order to reduce the needless shipping and returns mentioned in Part I. When considering a book's ability to be recycled, designers should avoid inks or coatings that impede a book's recyclability, some of which were mentioned in Part II.

Designing the Page

Designers can reduce a book's overall environmental impact by designing responsibly, meaning they can use the least amount of paper necessary when turning a manuscript into a readable object—a process that begins with layout. The margins are the frame of white space surrounding the main text block of a page and are determined to facilitate its readability. When oversized, margins can significantly increase a book's page count and subsequently its need for paper. While no single proportion is appropriate for all book margins, many designers consider the Golden Section (based on the golden ratio of 1:1.618) as a pinnacle of harmonious balance. Designers have revered this particular ratio since the Renaissance because of its resonance in various flora and fauna in the natural world, such as the spiral of nautilus and snail shells and the spiraled distribution of seeds in a sunflower. When margins are implemented using the Golden Section ratio, the text block accounts for approximately two-thirds of the page, while the remaining third is left blank. Many modern book designers respect the principles behind these margins, but have found that these proportions are financially irresponsible.

Layout decisions like the practice of starting new sections on rectos (the right-hand page of an open book) and the depth and placement of columns can also affect a book's page count. When new sections begin only on rectos, the spread's accompanying verso (left-hand page) may be left blank. This practice is fine if section openers fall evenly on rectos, but can cause unnecessary blank pages if each section's beginning is forced from a verso to a recto.

Line length refers to the number of characters on a single line of text. The number of characters per line affects readability. If a line's length is too short, the reader's eye will be forced to jump to the next line too frequently. If the length is too long, the eye can tire before it reaches the end of the line. In *The Elements of Typographic Style*, Robert Bringhurst defines the range of 45 to 75 characters per line as acceptable, and 66 characters in a single line as ideal. If a

Celery Design Collaborative

Based in Berkeley, California, Celery Design Collaborative specializes in approaching graphic design and branding strategies in a unique way. Instead of following a design from its beginning to its projected destination, Celery Design Collaborative traces it backwards to its conception in the studio. This process allows designers to consciously and creatively address potential hurdles they might encounter while infusing proactive, efficient solutions into the blueprint of each design. This process takes into consideration the life of the product even after they deliver it to their clients, extending to factors like the ecological impact of its packaging, distribution, and disposal. Celery recognizes the importance of examining the larger context in which their designs reside, taking into account what they refer to as upstream (relating to business strategy and marketing plans) and downstream (relating to materials, manufacturing, and distribution) to holistically determine the most sustainable design appropriate to each project.

Resources:
www.celerydesign.com

particular title has a larger trim size (e.g., 8.5"×11"), a designer may opt for a multiple-column design to keep line length manageable for the reader without leaving large amounts of unused space. This leads to a higher word count per page that then results in an overall reduction of page count. Typically, this practice is best suited for reference books and textbooks. The majority of fiction titles are printed on smaller trim sizes, such as 5.5"×8.5" and 6"×9", and are laid out with a single column that appropriately matches the page.

A book designer must also select a typeface that is highly readable and appropriate for the title. Many people are not aware that choosing a typeface is an important part of the design process, but even something as simple as a font choice can have environmental repercussions. For example, larger and thicker fonts, like Book Antiqua or Franklin Gothic, will not only require more ink than a lighter option but also tend to require more leading (or spacing) between lines to maintain a certain level of readability. This can lead to increased page counts that require more paper for each individual copy of the book. In 2010, a study conducted at the University of Wisconsin-Green Bay determined that Century Gothic used nearly 1.5% less ink coverage per page than their previous default font, Arial. While the reduction of ink usage is certainly good for the university's budgetary concerns, it can also decrease demand for non-renewable resources used in ink production if implemented on a larger scale. Additionally, decreased ink coverage can reduce the extent of the de-inking process during recycling.

Of course, if you don't find a font that suits you sustainably, you can make your own, which is what the Dutch firm SPRANQ did to extend the life of toner cartridges through ink coverage reduction. They developed Ecofont, a single Verdana-based font whose characters contain tiny holes in each stroke. These tiny holes, virtually unnoticeable in smaller font sizes, allow Ecofont to use 20% less ink than comparable typefaces. Currently, SPRANQ is developing software that will "punch holes" in any font, allowing designers to choose from a wide range of font families while using less ink. The Ecofont version of Arial, for example, can reduce ink usage by 26%.[59]

If a designer decides against altering an existing font, they can choose lighter weighted fonts and reduce the use of bold or black typefaces. These techniques not only decrease ink usage, but can increase line length and reduce the need for increased leading and margins without affecting readability. Choosing to use justified type also increases a page's word count and produces a more symmetrical and balanced page. Increasing the number of words on each page and eliminating unnecessary white space and blank pages can reduce a book's total page count, saving the necessary energy resources and wood fiber that go into the paper production process.

The presence of images, charts, and graphs in a text are more commonly found in nonfiction and technical titles. The overuse of these elements demands larger amounts of ink during printing and requires heavier weights of paper to prevent bleed-through. Let's consider a 5,000-copy print run of *The History of Everything,* which has a trim size of 6"×9" and is 256 pages long. The publisher decides that an overabundance of images requires an 80 lb. text stock. But if the design featured fewer images, the book might only demand the use of a 60 lb. text stock. The use of a heavier paper weight in this scenario would require nearly one ton more paper—roughly eight trees—than the lighter counterpart.[60]

Further environmental complications can arise if an image, text, or other decorative element is set flush against the edge of the page. To ensure a proper final product, printers must account for additional space around page edges for the ink to bleed onto, which requires a larger press sheet of paper. After the book has been printed, the extra paper is trimmed away, usually has no reuse option, and is typically sorted with make-ready as pre-consumer waste. If there is a high level of ink saturation on the paper, a more demanding de-inking process will be required during recycling, using more water, chemicals, energy, and time. The presence of interior page bleeds could potentially decrease the number of pages a printer can fit on a single press sheet, which would then increase the total amount of paper required for the print run, therefore only using interior bleeds when absolutely necessary is a good step toward designing sustainably.

Images, tables, and charts can be indispensable for some titles, and designers should judge an element's necessity on a case-by-case basis to avoid redundant tables and graphics. If these elements are necessary, designers should consider reducing their size and ink usage. Refraining from using 100% black backgrounds in tables, image frames, and in charts is one quick way to reduce ink coverage. This will also eliminate the need for heavier paper stocks necessary to prevent bleed-through.

Choosing the Trim Size

The size of a book not only determines the amount of paper necessary to produce the print run, but also the amount of paper wasted in the printing process. As mentioned in Part II, sheet-fed offset presses print on large sheets of a specific size that varies depending on the press itself and the printer's paper inventory. If there are no page bleeds on the book's interior, the pages can be laid out flush against one another, and press sheets are trimmed of excess paper along the outer margins. Some press sheet sizes are better suited for certain trim sizes in producing minimal waste. For example, if *The History of Everything* were printed on 60 lb. 23"×35" press sheets, 3.26

ECOFONT
ecofont

Ecofont

Several years ago, the Dutch design firm SPRANQ asked: How much of a letter can be removed while maintaining its readability? The answer resulted in the creation of Ecofont, a free font, in 2008. Ecofont is a font readable on both screen and in print. Its creation introduced a new way of printing. Ecofont attempts to address the problem of ink waste by essentially punching tiny circles of negative space into each character, which can reduce on average 25% of the ink used in traditional fonts. Ecofont is an innovative step in the right direction that confronts the challenge of creating sustainable, functional design options that are also aesthetically appealing.

Resources:
www.ecofont.com

tons of paper would be required to produce the book. The same run printed on 26"×40" press sheets would only use 2.64 tons of paper, a reduction of over half a ton of paper.[61] However, press sheet size is usually determined by a printer's press equipment and capabilities, so it is best to work closely with the printer to ensure minimal waste and maximum efficiency.

Deciding a book's trim size affects the total fiber use and paper waste during the printing process. For *The History of Everything*, reducing the trim size from 6"×9" to 5.5"×8.5" can save nearly half a ton of paper, or roughly four trees, depending on the press sheet size.[62] While there are some standardized book sizes in North America, the best way to determine the least wasteful trim size is by working directly with a printer. The printer may determine that a slightly nonstandard print size will increase the efficiency of the print run and decrease the total fiber use.

Using Colors and Decorative Elements

The number and types of colors used in a book's design can also affect the environmental impact of the print run. If the designer uses full color images on the book's cover or interior, a CMYK print run will be required. CMYK print runs use four ink colors: cyan (C), magenta (M), yellow (Y), and black (K). These four ink colors are combined or overlaid in various percentages to produce an extensive range of colors. If a book's cover or interior only calls for one or two specific colors, a designer may opt for **spot processes**. A spot process is a single, pre-formulated color ink, such as those standardized in the Pantone Matching System®. In offset printing, each single ink color—whether it is a spot process or one of the four inks used in CMYK printing—is typically run on a separate plate that must be cleaned after the print run. If a printing press is only capable of running one color at a time, then it may require a full cleanup after each individual ink run. This increases labor and resources used during the printing process and the amount of press cleaners required, which often release hazardous emissions into the air.

Certain ink colors may also contain hazardous compounds, such as heavy metals, in their pigments. Though the majority of CAMALS substances (cadmium, arsenic, mercury, antimony, lead, and selenium) have been removed from inks in North America, other toxic compounds may still be present in some pigments. Fluorescent and metallic inks generally have the highest proportions of these compounds and can contain copper and barium. Pigments mixed with the Pantone Warm Red mixing base include barium, while many pigments in blue or green inks contain copper. Additionally, many inks may contain cobalt as an additive, which assists with the drying process. During the paper recycling process, inks are removed and the resulting sludge is often disposed of into landfills. These toxic ingredients can eventually leech into local water supplies. When implementing single colors, it is better to choose a spot process over a mix of CMYK, as it only uses one ink instead of four separate inks. Designers can also obtain a **material safety data sheet** (MSDS) from ink manufacturers to determine the presence of any toxic compounds in a particular ink's pigment so that they may find a less toxic alternative.

Certain decorative elements added to books can increase the waste produced during a print run as well. Though they offer elegant or interesting flourishes, **French folds**, flaps, and pockets require larger press sheets that must be trimmed to the specified shape and size, resulting in additional paper usage and waste. These elements also increase a book's potential to be torn or bent. Damaged books returned by booksellers to publishers or distributors increase emissions related to

material safety data sheet (MSDS) | A form that describes the properties and hazards of a given chemical substance.

French folds | Two folds at right angles to one another. On a book cover, these are the front and back flaps that, when unfolded, extend beyond the trimmed book block.

life cycle analysis (LCA) | A measurement of a product's environmental impact throughout its usable life, from manufacturing through disposal.

transit. Depending on the extent of the damage, these books can be potentially pulped without ever having reached an end user. Foil stamping involves the application of a plastic film that carries pigment to paper. When metallic pigments are involved, they contain the same hazards as the pigments used in metallic inks. Additionally, foils that use a polyester film may render the underlying paper non-recyclable.

Some final decorative elements can be employed without hindering recycling or producing unnecessary additional waste. Die cutting involves removing segments of paper with a die, similar to a cookie cutter, without any additional chemicals or inks. However, designers must keep in mind that die cuts that are large or close to the edge of a page or cover may increase the book's potential to be damaged. Embossing and debossing involve pressing paper between metal dies, which give it a raised or lowered effect. This process does not attach any toxic substances to the paper and usually does not create a high potential for damage.

SustainAble, a book on sustainable graphic design by Aaris Sherin, is an excellent example of an innovative collaboration between design and printing to create a more sustainable finished product. This book's cover, demi-jacket, and endpapers were produced using its own make-ready and proof sheets, resulting in an interesting, aesthetically pleasing, and more efficient product.

Even if a particular book does not expressively demand sustainable design methods, designers can still implement many of these practices without sacrificing the book's overall aesthetic goals. Plus, sustainable strategies can be used as practical solutions to common problems: producing books that are less susceptible to damage will benefit the publisher, distributors, booksellers, and consumers. Sustainable design must also be effective design. If design standards are discarded for the sake of cramming words onto the page, then the entire project may be poorly received and result in a waste of both the publisher's efforts and the resources used to manufacture the book. Designers can build a network with others who employ sustainable practices as a resource for innovation, information, and ideas.

Digital Publishing

So you're at home re-reading your favorite book, and you find yourself savoring that lovely trifecta—the exquisite olfactory, tactile, and visual experience shared with bibliophiles as you inhale the used-book smell, touch the pages, and admire the cover art of that dog-eared paperback. This is not an uncommon sentiment, and it is no surprise that so many people share the idea that a book's value is bound up in its form and is not limited to its content. But, considering that last year alone over a million new titles were published in the U.S., how realistic and sustainable is this nostalgia when we start to factor in the environmental costs and the ever-growing ubiquity of technological advances in the publishing industry?[63]

Considering the environmental implications tied to the production of printed books, **e-books** may seem like a more sustainable solution at first glance. E-books not only eliminate the need for paper production, but also forgo the energy and resources necessary to manufacture and distribute printed books. However, these electronic files would be useless without an accompanying device, either a **dedicated device** (an e-reader) or a **multi-tasking device**. The resources needed to manufacture e-readers, the energy used to power individual devices and to store e-books on servers, and the e-reader's end-of-life destiny are all significant factors that deserve consideration when comparing digital production to print. By comparing projected **life cycle analyses** (LCA) of each format, along with other factors regarding accessibility and typical reading habits, publishers and consumers can see that digital publishing may not be as ecologically friendly as it might initially appear and that hidden drawbacks may potentially outweigh any advantages.

Environmental Advantages and Disadvantages of E-books

In our increasingly digital world, instant access to information has become not only a modern convenience but also an expectation. With electronic distribution, a reader can instantly access a text without traveling to a bookstore or waiting for a physical book to be shipped to her directly. As discussed in Part I, the carbon emissions of distribution and retail make up approximately 12.7% of the publishing industry's impact. The degree to which **digital distribution** offsets these emissions by forgoing physical transit altogether is small but not completely negligible.[64] That said, digital distribution reduces a book's environmental impact more efficiently than the use of alternative bio-based fuels for transportation by minimizing the transit of a physical book.

E-books provide an advantage when it comes to physical storage space, both on the part of the reader and the retailer. An e-book file itself takes up no physical space, and an e-reading device can store hundreds of these files in a container that is typically smaller and lighter than many single physical books. This saved storage space not only benefits the consumer; it also reduces necessary retail and warehouse space for storage by booksellers and distributors. The reduction of shelf space in bookstores and warehouses could potentially reduce the necessary energy used to power these buildings.

Though digital books do not require the physical space that printed books require, they must be stored on servers in order to provide access to consumers. When an e-book is purchased and downloaded, electricity is consumed and related emissions are released into the atmosphere. The internet may seem like an abstract source of unlimited data, but the environmental impact of accessing this information is tangible. In 2006, servers and data centers in the United States comprised 1.5% of all electricity consumption, or roughly 61 billion kilowatt-hours of electricity.[65] To put it in perspective, a single search on Google draws enough energy to release anywhere from one to ten grams of CO_2 emissions. In the United States alone, the number of Google searches performed each day average over 200 million, leading to a release of approximately 2,000 tons of CO_2 emissions daily.[66] This is roughly equivalent to the emissions released *per year* by 350 passenger vehicles.[67]

A physical book is subjected to regular wear and tear with each repeated use, which may eventually render it unusable. The repeated use of an e-book does not degrade the quality of the file. However, each repeated use of an e-book requires a supply of energy, whether it is from an e-reading device's battery or from an AC adapter. On the other hand, the number of times a printed book is accessed does not add to its total emissions. Nearly all of a printed book's environmental impacts are tied directly to its production and distribution, not its continued use.

Powering e-reading devices and computers used to read e-books involves energy needs. The e-book's lack of physical form may make it seem infinitely sustainable since the file itself can never end up in a landfill, but the disposal of an e-reading device contributes to the growing environmental impact of **e-waste**. Waste produced by electronic devices, or e-waste, has become a considerable social and environmental problem around the world. Because of the rapidly growing technology industry, electronic devices of all sorts are constantly entering the marketplace at an increasing rate. Consumers purchasing these new devices often dispose of their previous devices, many of which are still fully functional. Of all the e-waste produced in the United States each year, nearly 50%–80% is exported to developing countries—including China, India, Ghana, and Nigeria—where it often ends up in landfills, contaminating the land, water, and air of some of the world's poorest people.[68] Copper, silicon, and iron can be harvested during recycling and resold; however, there is often little regulation of disposal and recycling in these countries. The presence of toxic materials in these devices and the burden of growing landfills can quickly overshadow any potential benefits.

polyvinyl chloride
(PVC)| A chlorinated
plastic that was
once common in
the manufacturing
process of electronic
devices. Vinyl chloride
monomer (VCM)—a
basic component
of PVC—is highly
toxic, carcinogenic,
and even explosive.
When incinerated,
PVC releases dioxins
into the surrounding
atmosphere.

brominated flame
retardants (BFRs)| A
bromine-based
polymer applied to
electronic products
to reduce their
flammability. These
compounds are
lipophilic and bioac-
cumulative, meaning
they accumulate and
are stored in the fat
cells of humans and
other animals. Their
toxicity can cause
negative effects in
digestive, endocrine,
and nervous systems.

Electronic devices and e-waste can contain an array of toxic substances, including heavy metals, **polyvinyl chloride** (PVC), and **brominated flame retardants** (BFRs). If present in landfills, these toxic substances can contaminate local groundwater. If the waste is incinerated, dioxins and other hazardous air pollutants are emitted into the air. Heavy metals, such as lead and mercury, can cause significant damage to the kidneys and nervous system. The incineration of PVC releases dioxins into the atmosphere. Also, many PVC products contain phthalate plasticizers that can damage the endocrine system. BFRs are resistant to degradation and their toxic components are bioaccumulative, meaning they build up in the bodies of humans, animals, and other organisms.[69] During manufacturing and recycling processes, workers come in close contact with all of these toxic materials.

Comparing Life Cycles

The most accurate way of examining the environmental impact of e-books against printed books is to examine life cycle analyses of each format. The e-book file itself is intangible and must be accessed using a device—whether it is a dedicated e-reader or a personal computer—so comparing two concrete elements is both appropriate and practical.

In 2003, Greg Kozak compared the life cycles of e-books and printed books for the Center of Sustainable Systems at the University of Michigan. Kozak chose to conduct research based on the use of textbooks by college students. He compared the purchase and usage of forty printed textbooks—an average purchased by a student over a four-year span—against forty electronic books read on one e-reading device over the same four-year span. Kozak traced each format through every aspect of its production and the student's usage of each type of book. Kozak determined that the majority of a printed book's environmental impact comes from its manufacturing process, while the majority of the impact associated with the e-reading device stemmed from constant use. In Table 4, the three major forms of environmental impact examined in Kozak's study are presented, showing the advantages and disadvantages of each reading system.

Table 4. A Comparison Between the Major Forms of Environmental Impact in a Traditional Printed Book System and an E-reader System[70]

Type of Impact	Global Warming Gases (measured in CO_2 equivalents	Stratospheric Ozone Depletion (measured in CFC-11 equivalents)	Acidification (measured in SO_2 equivalents)
Traditional Book System	218 kg	1.04 E-06kg	1.09 kg
E-Reader System	60 kg	1.14 E-06kg	0.39 kg

In August of 2009, the Cleantech Group released an LCA of the Amazon Kindle 2 with slightly different results. The study claims that a Kindle 2 will produce roughly 168 kg of CO_2 equivalents over a four-year life span, which the report equivocates to 22.5 printed books. However, the study also projects that reading three e-books each month instead of purchasing the same three printed books could save 1,074 kg of CO_2 equivalents over the same four-year span.[71] Another recent life cycle analysis of an e-reading device determined that the purchase of 100 e-books instead of printed books would offset the purchase of Apple's iPad.[72]

As with Kozak's study, the Cleantech group's report seems to agree that e-reading devices are a clear frontrunner as far as greenhouse gas emissions are concerned. However, both of these studies assume that the reader will fully switch to e-books after purchasing an e-reading device. Though e-books have become increasingly popular in the past few years, any claim that they will completely replace printed books may be somewhat of an overstatement. A consumer's hesitance about the switch is attributable not only to the discomfort of trading familiarity with printed books for an entirely new format, but also to the fact that there are still many printed titles without an electronic equivalent. If a reader purchases an e-reading device but continues to purchase printed books regularly, the device only increases the consumer's own carbon footprint. However, in the United States, an average of only ten books were sold per person in 2006.[73] If this is reflective of national book purchasing habits, it would take 2.25 years to offset a single Kindle 2 device and 14.4 years to reach the 1,074 kg of CO_2 equivalent savings. E-reading devices may remain fully functional for two years but will likely not last 14.4 years in order to attain such a significant offset of greenhouse gases.

This leads to another major issue with e-readers: their average life span and end-of-life destiny. While printed books can remain intact for decades (centuries, even), electronic devices tend to break down or become outdated after a few years. E-reading devices, like all technology, come with a **built-in obsolescence** factor. For example, Amazon released the first generation Kindle in October 2007, only to release the Kindle 2 fifteen months later in February 2009. Subsequently, consumers who wish to own the most up-to-date technology will contribute more waste to the growing accumulation of electronic devices in landfills.

The primary (and sometimes, only) function of a dedicated e-reading device is the display of e-books in whichever file format it supports (e.g., PDF, EPUB, MOBI, etc.). Purchasing separate electronic devices for different functions, such as reading e-books, browsing the web, or maintaining calendars and contacts, can substantially increase a consumer's carbon footprint. For this reason, multitasking devices—such as the Apple iPad, smartphones, or laptops—may prove to be a more sustainable option since they have a variety of functions other than reading e-books. However, manufacturers of dedicated e-readers are increasingly adapting to the multitasking trend. In order to remain competitive in the e-reader market, companies are rapidly developing web browsers and mobile applications for their devices. While multitasking devices are superior to their dedicated counterparts, many still do not match the functionality of the laptop and desktop computers that consumers will likely continue to own in addition to their new device.

E-books and the Publishing Industry

E-books and e-readers are throwing the publishing industry for a loop, as anyone who follows publishing news will know. Pricing wars, format debates, skyrocketing sales, new devices—every day brings something new. With an industry in such flux, we can do little but report and predict, but predicting the future is not an exact science. We can discuss opportunities we see and how we might take advantage of them, but every publisher and every book is different. The discussion needs to move away from Books, with a capital B, and toward how to best present a story. Publishing is, as we defined in the introduction to this book, the process of making literature and information available for public view. Just as we talked about in the Acquisitions & Editing chapter earlier, truly sustainable publishing begins with acquisition. The discussion is just broader now: is this piece of literature destined for print (and why) or digital (and why)? That's the big picture, but just as there are smaller steps we can take to reduce paper consumption, there are smaller steps that the digital realm can help us take.

The use of e-reading devices reduces in-house paper flow for publishers. Making copies of paper manuscripts can become both cumbersome and wasteful. Manuscripts can be accepted in a digital format and accessed by editors through e-reading devices and computers. Digital manuscripts can also allow for more streamlined collaboration among editors and production managers. Additionally, the use of electronic manuscripts can allow marketers and salespersons to easily access multiple manuscripts on one device instead of having separate copies of printed manuscripts. However, implementing this type of workflow is not without its roadblocks. For this type of system to be a fruitful one, publishers would need to purchase more advanced e-reading devices that would allow primary editing functions, such as changing text and placing comments. Laptops are also an option here, though they are generally more expensive. Publishers would not only need to train their editorial staff to use these new devices, but would also need continuous and efficient training to keep up with the most current technology.

The digital book can also offer an increased profit margin for publishers and a lower retail price for consumers. Though creating an e-book file requires some additional production, an e-book, unlike a physical book, has no material cost related to print production. Traditionally, a publisher figures the cost of the book based on all in-house, pre-production expenses plus all out-of-house production costs like printing, shipping, and distribution fees, and then passes these costs on to the consumer. E-books have none of the associated printing or shipping costs, which, in the print world, make up most of the book's cost. Currently, most e-books can be purchased for less than the retail cost of a physical book. A reduced price point makes it easier for the consumer to justify buying the e-reading device required to read these books. It also reflects the fact that production costs of an e-book are much lower. However, the drop in retail price for an e-book may result in significant complications for publishers. An industry as large as publishing has difficulty adjusting to rapidly evolving market demands and smaller profits. Even if the profit margins are higher on e-book sales, the retail price is lower. Over the past few years, publishing houses and e-book retailers have argued over price ceilings for e-books. Big retailers like Amazon have argued for lower prices to drive sales of their dedicated device, while publishers worry that this may devalue their investment in an author's work and also the established retail price of the printed books.

E-books and Consumers

For consumers, there are many advantages to e-books (like the lower price point discussed above), but there are other hidden complications and drawbacks that should be considered in any larger discussion of sustainability issues.

Interactive elements that exist in e-books are an advantage without a true equivalent in printed books. For example, a reader can access hyperlinks that allow him to jump to specific places in the text or to external sites through a web browser, which is especially useful for texts with many footnotes or endnotes. This technology also allows publishers to set up websites with content that is less suitable for an e-book format but can be made easily accessible with a link placed in the e-book file. While indexes in the back of printed books allow points of reference for readers searching for certain subjects, many e-reading devices allow readers to search the entire text for specific words and phrases. Some e-reading devices can even support more advanced HTML5 and Flash elements, such as interactive images and videos. E-reading devices also allow text enlargement for those who have difficulty reading small type, doing away with the need for separate large print editions of printed books. Some e-readers even support text-to-speech technology, which could eventually mean the end of audiobooks as a separate entity.

Because of the ease with which they can be updated, e-books prove themselves to be an especially viable alternative for periodicals and textbooks. Publishers can simply change the outdated information and send the updated files to their distributor and retailers without having to order a new print run for the updated text. This can also be a benefit to consumers of expensive reference or textbooks, as the digital book is generally lower in price than the physical form.

In spite of all the technological benefits of e-books, many readers still express discomfort with adjusting to a different format. Printed books have been an established means of communicating information for hundreds of years. Though some denounce this preference while encouraging readers to adapt to a format that has the potential to be more sustainable, it is still a valid concern. One common consumer complaint refers to an aversion to reading on-screen. To alleviate this concern some e-reading devices use electronic ink (or **e-ink**) **displays** that, unlike typical light-emitted diode (or LED) **backlit displays**, do not require backlighting, which makes them easier to read in sunlight and reduces strain on the eyes. E-readers such as

Digital Rights Management (DRM)| An access control technology that limits the use and/or sharing of digital content, like e-books and digital music files. DRM is often a controversial topic since it has both benefits (such as the prevention of piracy) and downfalls (preventing a legal owner from accessing previously purchased content on a newer device).

the original Barnes & Noble Nook and the lines of Sony Readers and Amazon Kindles all use e-ink displays. These types of displays change through electrophoresis, a process in which charged titanium dioxide display particles are suspended in conductive fluid that react to voltage emitted from panels beneath the display. This means such devices only draw power when the display is refreshed (such as when a reader "turns" an electronic "page"). Backlit LED displays, on the other hand, require a constant source of power to display an image or text and are used in most laptops, Apple's iPad, and Barnes & Nobles' NookColor. Because e-readers with e-ink displays do not require constant power, a consumer would not need to charge the device quite as much as they would for one using an LED backlit display.

While digital books may have positive environmental and economic attributes, some of the social impacts are more difficult to quantify. Unlike e-books, the printed book can be shared easily among friends, checked out repeatedly from libraries, and sold through used bookstores after its initial consumer has finished with it, all of which are common practices that are more difficult to track than straightforward book sales. Because of the high potential for piracy, many e-books come with a set of **Digital Rights Management** (DRM) restrictions. These restrictions can make it impossible for the e-book to be shared among friends and can even prevent the paying consumer from accessing the file on more than one device. Because of their potential for unauthorized replication, e-books cannot currently be resold in the same manner as printed books.

When considering e-books as a replacement for printed books, it is necessary to consider the accessibility of each format. Printed books stand alone without the need for a costly electronic device to view them. Currently, the retail prices for e-books are not significantly lower than market paperbacks, making the purchase of an e-reading device difficult to offset for those with less disposable income. (While the price margin between an e-book and its hardcover counterpart is significantly larger, one would still need to purchase dozens of e-book versions to offset the cost of their e-reading device.) Printed books can be easily accessed for free through local library systems. Though most libraries have implemented digital catalogs, the files are still not accessible to those without the necessary device. If readers were able to check out electronic devices the way they can currently check out printed books, there would likely need to be some sort of collateral to cover the potential damage or theft of such a costly device. This collateral is something that not every person is capable of providing, which again impedes the accessibility of the digital format. If the driving force behind books—both electronic and printed—is to share information with any audience who wishes to access it, then the prohibitive cost of e-readers is a major problem and a social justice issue that should be thoroughly considered before consumers, governments, and publishers rush into a paperless world. The triple bottom line principle states that sustainability encompasses not only the preservation of natural and economic capital, but also human capital. Without widespread accessibility, e-books cannot truly be deemed socially sustainable.

Making E-books a Viable Alternative

One of the first steps in improving the sustainability of electronic devices is examining how the materials are procured, how they are used during manufacturing, and how they are disposed. A solution that encompasses both the original sources of device components and e-waste accumulation issues would be the use of recycled materials in electronics manufacturing. It takes a great deal more energy to procure and refine glass, plastic, and metal components from virgin sources than it does to use recycled materials during production.

For example, the Environmental Protection Agency (EPA) estimates that the recycling of one million laptops would save enough electricity to power 3,657 homes in the United States for a full year.[74] Unfortunately, out of the 2.25 million tons of electronics discarded in 2007, only 18% were recycled, while the remaining 82% ended up in landfills.[75] Because of the presence of toxic materials in e-waste, it is vital that electronics recycling facilities practice proper disposal of non-recyclable parts and high safety standards for workers. Third-party accreditation programs, such as the EPA's Responsible Recycling Practices and Basel Action Network's (BAN) e-Stewards Program, ensure that facilities operate in a way that is socially, economically, and environmentally responsible.

A few electronics manufacturers are already including post-consumer waste plastics and other alternative materials in the production

Basel Action Network (BAN)

Basel Action Network (BAN), a nonprofit based in Seattle, Washington, is the world's only organization specifically committed to confronting the far-reaching devastation caused by toxic trade—toxic wastes, products, and technologies—and concomitant issues of human rights and environmental justice. By confronting these problems at a macro level, BAN works to simultaneously prevent disproportionate environmental toxic practices and promote sustainable solutions such as improving trade regulations, encouraging responsible manufacturing processes, reducing the use of toxic chemicals, and encouraging the democratic design of consumer products to reflect sustainable choices. BAN is dedicated to the preservation and implementation of the United Nation's treaty, the Basel Convention on the Control of Transboundary Movements of Hazardous Wastes and Their Disposal, and the Basel Ban Amendment, a 1998 decision that effectively bans all forms of hazardous waste exports from the wealthiest industrialized countries. The BAN's mission is to prevent the export of toxic waste from rich countries to poorer countries, and to define globally responsible toxic waste management of electronics and obsolete shipping vessels. BAN's advocacy includes its e-Stewardship Initiative (identifying globally responsible e-recyclers via an accredited certification program) and its Shipbreaking Campaign.

Resources:
http://www.ban.org
www.e-stewards.org

of certain devices. In April 2010, Lenovo launched the ThinkPad L Series laptop line. These machines are made with an overall post-consumer waste content of 18%, the highest amount of any laptop in the industry.[76] Recycled plastic casings are not the only sustainable option in consumer electronics. Since 2007, Asus has been manu-facturing a series of laptops with bamboo casing. The u6v Bamboo and u2e Bamboo have a series of separate bamboo panels that can be detached and replaced individually if necessary, decreasing the need to discard the entire system for minor damages. Bamboo is a highly renewable resource and is biodegradable. Though Asus's Bamboo series does include some plastic in its inner casings, the overall reduc-tion of plastic can reduce hazardous emissions during manufacturing and put less of a strain on the influx of e-waste in landfills.

Some electronics manufacturers have started to implement solar power technology into the production process in order to decrease energy consumption. lg has created a prototype e-reader that has a thin solar panel that can charge the device for an entire day's worth of reading over the span of a few hours.[77] The solar power trend is thriving throughout the field of portable electronics; for example, both Sharp and Samsung have developed solar-powered cell phones. As the presence of solar power in the electronics market continues to grow, durable solar panels could potentially eliminate the need to charge devices with electricity sourced from nonrenewable resources.

If digital books are to become a more sustainable option than printed books, the manufacturers of e-reading devices must take into account the triple bottom line. According to the Grassroots Recycling Network, the concept of **Extended Producer Responsibility** (epr) requires manufacturers to accept physical and financial responsibility for the impacts of their products throughout their entire life cycle, starting with their initial design. The existing lca comparisons of e-devices and printed books cite e-device lifespans that are poten-tially twice as long as electronic devices actually last. By choosing to make devices durable and long-lasting, electronics manufacturers can provide a viable alternative that can reduce the harvesting of virgin fiber, energy, and emissions associated with the production of printed books. Additionally, these manufacturers should fully disclose detailed information on their production process in order to provide a layer of transparency so consumers can make informed decisions. E-reader manufacturers like Apple and Sony have released reports on their products' environmental impacts and have committed to eliminate harmful chemical compounds such as PVC and BFRS. Manufacturers should also offer direct recycling programs that ensure the reuse of appropriate materials and the proper disposal of toxic components. Both Apple and Amazon offer such programs, and many electronics manufacturers refurbish slightly dysfunctional devices for resale. With time, the elimination of unnecessary waste, dangerous emissions, and excess energy consumption could make reading on electronic devices a more sustainable alternative to print.

While neither digital nor printed books are perfectly sustainable, each provides their own set of benefits to the world of publishing. Using a combination of e-books and paper books will be vital to the success of future publishers and to the long-term sustainability of the industry. Certain titles may work better as e-books, while others should be printed. The rapidly transforming landscape of the book industry demands that we re-examine what constitutes the most responsible vehicle by which the content of books are read and that we determine which vehicle is most appropriate for specific content and audience.

E-books might be a viable solution for material that shouldn't (arguably) ever see the printed page. Books containing information that becomes quickly outdated—such as the information found in some textbooks—are excellent candidates for this format. Digital books may also serve as a viable sustainable alternative to mass-market paperbacks. These titles are often overproduced due to their popularity and make up a significant amount of bookseller returns and landfill waste. Most e-book bestseller charts are composed of titles printed in this format. Consumers of mass-market paperbacks, especially romance novels, are starting to embrace e-books as well. In late 2010, romance had become the fastest-growing segment of the e-book market.[78] If publishers choose to cut mass market print runs and offer titles digitally instead, the savings of paper and resources that go into book production could be significant enough to offset some of the negative impacts of e-reading device production.

Technological advances within the publishing industry are transforming the vehicle by which we read the content of books and are altering the very notion of the book as a tangible artifact. Regardless of manufacturers' initiatives to improve their electronic devices, print books are still significantly more accessible than their digital counterparts. Eventually, perhaps, technology like e-readers will become increasingly sustainable—economically, environmentally, *and* socially—and could someday prove to be as ubiquitous as printed books.

Marketing

Book marketing is the process by which publishers define the audience for a book and develop a strategy to tell audience members about the book to enhance and support sales efforts. The values of sustainability and those of traditional marketing practices could appear to stand in direct conflict with each other, but they don't have to. Marketing can seem nebulous and intangible, but it also tends to involve a large amount of resources that can generate enormous waste if efforts are not conducted in a thoughtful and sustainable manner. Marketing books can be done without flooding mailboxes with paper resources. In fact, embracing more responsible practices can be an excellent selling point for a publishing house. This section will explore marketing both in terms of book marketing and more broadly in terms of general company marketing, although the two can have a symbiotic relationship. This section will also discuss auditing, which can be employed as a valuable marketing tool to promote publishing houses and to promote individual books.

Book marketing

Strong marketing remains pivotal to a book's success; a good book typically cannot survive poor marketing, and rarely is a book so

BLAD (basic layout and design)| A sample of a book's interior design, used for marketing purposes.

galleys| Promotional copies of a book's manuscript used for marketing and reviewing purposes. At this point, the manuscript has typically undergone some editing and typesetting, but is not yet finalized for full print production.

successful that it does not need strong marketing. It's very tempting to think that publishing is about selling books to bookstores and that that's where the relationship ends. This paradigm is outdated; in the past there were fewer media outlets and fewer avenues for book marketing, but now people don't rely so extensively on bookstores and book reviews to find out about new titles.

A publisher's marketing and sales departments are typically involved with a book from the moment a manuscript is considered for acquisition. Their input on the book's prospects in the marketplace are an essential part of the decision-making process that goes on before an author signs a contract with a publisher. Once the book is acquired, they decide where to direct their marketing efforts and what type of **marketing collateral** is appropriate to produce. Because of their knowledge of the industry, marketing teams also play a large role in shaping other major aspects of a book, such as the style or tone based on demographical targeting, the retail price, and the size of a print run based on market demands. Standard marketing collateral includes branded logo merchandise, advertising material, and promotional products. It's not surprising that most marketing material in publishing traditionally comes in the form of paper and ink: bookmarks, shelf-talkers, posters, postcards, marketing plans, catalogs, tip sheets, cover letters (used during the review process when soliciting a blurb, review, or article), sales sheets, BLADs, **galleys**, life-size cut-outs of well-known writers, etc. These items add to the constant consumption of paper, ink, and toner used in the production of a book. Book marketers can reduce these environmental excesses by asking the right questions, such as:

- How effective is this marketing material?
- Could it be just as effective (if not more so) in a digital form?
- Is the material appropriate for the targeted audience?
- How can this material be produced more sustainably?
- What are the real costs of this material (triple bottom line thinking)?
- Can the same message reach the intended audience through other, non-material means?

Publishers can also approach businesses and individuals they work with and request that they shift to electronic invoices and correspondence. If mailing material is necessary, there are options that use fewer resources to convey information. Postcards, for example, can be printed with vegetable-based inks on paper or chipboard made from reclaimed paper stock with a high post-consumer waste content. It can be productive to talk with a printer and see if make-ready materials are available for products like bookmarks or business cards.

By updating its mailing list frequently, a company can avoid sending collateral to duplicate or undeliverable addresses. In addition, always offering the option of receiving communications electronically to reduce paper and postage will help in the reduction of waste. Even in using paper, companies can integrate sustainable design into products and help to dramatically reduce the environmental impact of marketing.

Galleys are an important element of book marketing. Produced in advance of a book's publication, galleys contain the complete (often un-proofed) manuscript with all its necessary marketing information and can be sent to reviewers, websites, book distributers, libraries, journalists, and others who might promote the book. A viable alternative to mailing these printed galleys is to distribute them in e-book or PDF format, which is less expensive, much faster, and far less wasteful. E-galleys also allow the book publisher to reach audiences that they might not otherwise have been able to include due to time or budget constraints, like international markets, smaller publications, peripheral reviewers, and independent bookstores. Using a combination of electronic and printed galleys will allow the publisher to reduce waste and expand the galley's recipients while still reaching all the necessary targets.

Press kits are another marketing tool that could be most sustainable in electronic form. A typical press kit might include an author's bio, details about the book, additional publicity information, reviews, bookmarks, postcards, and posters. Tailoring press kits to appropriately fit the target person or business can result in conserving materials. The presentation of promotional material in electronic press kits also contains the potential for greater creativity. As a digital file, it can store the same informative material as its hard copy counterpart but with interactive elements. Once created, it can be emailed, burned to a CD or DVD, uploaded on memory devices, or opened as a website, easily facilitating the process of sharing and distributing the information. The benefits of providing press kits and galleys in electronic form are enormous; in addition to offering flexibility and versatility, press kits and galleys in electronic form involve comparatively little financial cost or environmental impact.

On September 28, 2010, the global market research company Ipsos OTX MediaCT released a study that found that people ages 13 to 74 spend half their waking hours interacting with media.[79] This is good news for book publishing—but books by nature have a much higher barrier of entry than other media. They are not as cheap as much of their competing media; reading is time consuming; the market is so oversaturated with hundreds of thousands of new titles that deciding what books to buy can be a daunting choice; and more than ever, publishers have to competitively vie for their audiences' time with other forms of media. Book marketers must avoid selling a disposable relationship between their readers and their books, and strive instead for cultivating long-term, loyal readers. The more opportunities to engage readers with the book in this lasting way, the greater the marketing potential, and this often requires utilizing other forms of media.

Readers are often overwhelmed by the sheer number of published books available and can find themselves perplexed by what to read next. There's great opportunity for marketers to facilitate quick, easily perusable ways to explore potential books in a way that involves minimal environmental impact. Book trailers™, or video advertisements for books that employ techniques similar to those of movie trailers, offer one such option, but they can be expensive to produce, and a current lack of ubiquity makes searching for titles difficult unless a reader knows what he or she is looking for. One day, however, book trailers might become as common and effective as movie trailers. The website Bookscreening.com is one example of a response to this growing market, and offers book lovers a collection of organized, easily navigated trailers, a forum to discuss the trailers, and an option to share them. It also provides authors and publishers with a hub for announcing new releases of book trailers and receiving feedback from readers.

Pinball Publishing

Founded by Laura and Austin Whipple in 2002, Pinball Publishing is a printing facility in Portland, Oregon, with a low-impact business model that reflects their commitment to provide high quality, environmentally responsible printing. Pinball specializes in custom offset printing, which emphasizes spot color printing over the traditional four-color process. They focus on using 100% recycled paper (most of which contains FSC-certified fiber), printing with vegetable-based inks, and utilizing alcohol-free dampening systems and solvents and solutions with low levels of VOCs. Additionally, 100% of their electric bill supports energy from renewable resources. Pinball has used their print production expertise to develop customizable printed items that take advantage of efficient paper yields and wasteless production cycles.

Resources:
http://viewerslikeu.squarespace.com/main/2008/7/7/interview-pinball-publishing.html
www.pinballpublishing.com

Online marketing has become an essential part of a book marketer's strategy. Publishers have begun investing more resources in online marketing, networking, and creating audience loyalty by branding, word of mouth, and viral marketing techniques. The internet is an invaluable tool in marketing; utilizing digital media is a quicker and more efficient way of reaching a wide range of people and businesses at very little cost. Also, the reality is that in a more competitive marketplace, publishers can no longer afford to ignore an untapped online audience.

Beyond the basics of maintaining a strong, informative, and interesting website and offering online press releases, viral marketing techniques use social networks and generally don't cost a lot of money overall—just time and energy. Utilizing social media like Facebook, Twitter, Flickr, podcasts, and author-run blogs allows authors and publishers to achieve virtually paperless marketing tactics that foster a high degree of interactive audience participation. These sites allow authors and publishers to provide instantaneous updates about relevant news; spread this information virally; establish a direct relationship with readers and potential readers; and explore creative ways to captivate the interest of a diverse audience. Book marketing involves sophisticated salesmanship, and ultimately is part of the broader entertainment industry. Every prototypical reader is also a media omnivore who must filter through a staggering amount of sensory input from newspapers, magazines, advertisements, billboards, television, movies, radio, podcasts, and the internet. The contemporary book marketer's challenge is to find a way to efficiently compete with all this while using resources as responsibly and sustainably as possible.

According to the theory of panarchy, the key to sustaining any system is diversity, and the same is true in green marketing. Increasing one's online presence and marketing strategies allows the use of less physical collateral and marketing products, and ideally would allow the publisher to redirect that budget toward greener products.

Company Marketing

Integrating sustainable practices into each step of a book's life cycle (including marketing) will not go unnoticed by the public or the publishing industry at large. Publishers should consider how their marketing and their sustainable practices could mutually enhance one another. One of the first decisions a publisher needs to make is how to publicly treat the role of sustainability within the company. It can be a smart strategy to go public with the commitment to environmental stewardship, but only after the publishing house has a proven track record in sustainable efforts with solid data to support claims. For example, this might mean calculations of how their decision to use a particular type of paper for their most recent title contributed to a 7,600-pound reduction in carbon dioxide equivalent of greenhouse gases, a 9-ton reduction in virgin fiber use (the equivalent of about 65 trees), a 1,845-pound reduction in solid waste, and a 30,226-gallon reduction in wastewater. The above example is only the tip of the iceberg for the type of data a publisher might track to demonstrate the impact of sustainable choices. A company's commitment to sustainability can be used as both a promotional tool and a model to effect change in the industry. Such visible changes will likely encourage sustainable publishing practices in other companies.

Incorporating educational outreach is one powerful marketing tool that also embraces social sustainability. For example, staff at a publishing house might volunteer monthly in local elementary schools to talk to students about some of the behind-the-scenes things that go into making books, and educate them about steps they take to lessen the environmental impact of the process. These efforts not only enhance the well-being of the community, but also gain exposure for the press and might catch the media's attention. Considering a collaborative partnership with local green businesses can also create a stronger community, so that companies do not simply exist as isolated sustainable brands, but rather contribute as part of a larger, socially sustainable system. Such a practice also demonstrates a commitment to sustainability through involvement in a larger network and serves the double purpose of increasing awareness of environmentally friendly practices and alternatives while generating positive publicity in a way that might reach a different audience than conventional book marketing outreach.

But caution is necessary when gauging how far-reaching sustainable efforts actually extend. It is important to verify that a company's claims match its actions. If a publishing house markets itself as "green," sustainability should be reflected in the actual production of every book, marketing venture, and office practices. If a company doesn't have the means or resources to implement sustainability to this degree, it might consider starting small with a commitment to consistently increase sustainable practices. Perhaps this means creating an imprint that is specifically dedicated to integrating sustainable design and printing into a series of books, while continuing efforts to systematically improve the rest of the press. Environmentally friendly publishers can apply marketing techniques to communicate their corporate responsibility and sustainable practices to the public.

If a publishing house or editing firm integrates sustainable practices into their production and office practices but still employs conventional marketing practices that involve vast waste, it runs the risk of losing credibility if publicly claiming to be "green." It is wise to consider green marketing as a reflection of all the measures taken in actual book production. The transition to responsible, sustainable practices should not be a decision made solely for marketing value—it should be a reflection of practices that demonstrates this commitment.

The overuse of words such as *green* and *sustainable* have dulled public opinion of their meaning and are often indiscriminately tacked on to marketing campaigns. It is important for companies to avoid greenwashing or disingenuously representing themselves to the public. A simple, succinct statement of purpose that is grounded in specific facts will hopefully avoid trendy, vague statements that risk misleading customers. When possible, it is advisable to replace generic statements such as "We are a sustainable company," with concrete examples and data that substantiate these claims and demonstrate active, sustainable efforts. Setting these standards for the public to see commits a company to certain actions and invites scrutiny. Failing to live up to promises will cause a company to lose the trust of its audience and consumers. Some place high value on third-party verified symbols and accredited certifications, like those from the Forest Stewardship Council and the Sustainable Forestry Initiative (discussed in Part II), but it is important to keep in mind that not all certifications are as credible as others.

Other steps include establishing a company committee responsible for staying informed on current sustainability research, as well as tracking and analyzing the materials and processes in action. By educating its staff, a publishing house can become more aware of which company measures are in place to avoid greenwashing when promoting those issues to the public. A commitment to transparency allows employees and consumers alike to have easy access to information regarding decisions made about methods and practices within a company through **self-auditing**.

Marketing & Audits

An important measure publishers and designers can take to avoid greenwashing is to institute a self-auditing system that can be applied to both specific projects and long-term progress. A strong audit openly shares information about a company's practices and consumption, ideally encouraging like-minded businesses to seek similar sustainable practices. Transparency is the key here; even when an audit reveals a company's weaker areas, it can guide others who also strive to improve. There's no equation or formula for an exemplar audit that reflects sustainable publishing choices; each company's process for creating audits will be unique to their needs and practices and might evolve as they discover better methods of presenting this information or improve their practices.

An audit might provide concrete data on the impacts of each print run for a given book. The audit at the beginning of this book shows one potential format for conveying information about *Rethinking Paper & Ink*'s particular print run. Sustainable printing is a rapidly evolving industry, so by researching printers ahead of time and maintaining close contact with a printer's representatives, a publisher can stay as up-to-date as possible on the most current and sustainable options. Conducting thorough research is key—not just on paper, ink, glue, cleaner, and press models, but also on energy sources for the production of these materials; chemicals and waste incurred; distances between your printer and your distributor; and the companies and manufacturers that produce the materials. All of this should be considered when selecting a printer. It's also beneficial to note any accredited certifications held by the printer and paper and ink manufacturers. These types of labels inform consumers that the product adheres to high industry standards acknowledged by a trustworthy third party. For example, paper certifications might convey important information about the paper itself, the manner in which the trees were harvested, and how the paper was responsibly manufactured at the paper mill (see Part II).

Calculating every aspect of every factor of the production process is currently not possible. However, the Environmental Defense Fund's paper calculator offers a comparative analysis of not only the reduction of virgin pulp through PCW-recycled options, but also other impacts, such as greenhouse gasses, wastewater, and hazardous air pollutants. Re-nourish is another organization that provides these waste calculations and is more hands-on with the project's design specifications. Their calculator has input areas for press sheet size, trim size, printer margins, and bleeds, in addition to suggesting ways to slightly alter these factors to save even more paper.

For self-audits to be effective, it is crucial to remain informed and to be honest about decisions made. Audits ultimately reflect very complex tradeoffs based on decisions made in the process—in some instances, this means having to sacrifice certain sustainable options for less sustainable ones, and audits should reveal these shortcomings, along with any gaps in information. Choosing printers and manufacturers who are also transparent about their processes tends to work best, but sometimes all of these details can still be difficult to find.

The usefulness of auditing goes beyond company walls. In some way, audits from multiple publishing houses on comparable titles, or audits for multiple projects within a single publishing house, could function as a barometer for the current state of the industry. For example, several different publishers might produce audits on the sustainable printing of their books that all reveal a lack of information on the ink used, demonstrating a general need for ink manufacturers to be more transparent about their production and to have the components and levels of toxicity of their ink more readily accessible.

Likewise, a cross-examination of audits from different publishers might show that every time any of them use a particular printer, the PCW content of the paper used is consistently lower than would be ideal, perhaps revealing accessibility issues due to prices. According to *The Business Guide to Sustainability*, in situations when preferred materials aren't available in reliable quantities "or production is at such a low level that costs are prohibitively expensive…the industrial infrastructure is not yet there to track chain of custody. The only way to solve this problem is to partner with those in the industry; roll up your sleeves and figure it out collaboratively. Long-term purchasing commitments build confidence in potential suppliers that making sustainable investments pays off."[80] In this way, audits have the ability to both reflect current practices and indicate growing demands in the industry that might anticipate an expanding market for, say, aqueous coatings or higher percentages of vegetable-based inks.

Home and Office Practices

Change starts with the individual. Even without the authority to change the overall system, there are many simple office maintenance tasks that can be implemented to make the home or office more sustainable. Reducing paper consumption, making more responsible printing choices, and encouraging sustainable changes in the practices of others are a few such changes. The following list offers tips to lessen the negative environmental and social impacts of publishing while cultivating an economically sustainable business.

Suggested Office Practices

- In cold weather, set the thermostat to the lowest tolerable temperature and wear more clothes to save energy.
- Provide clearly marked bins for plastics, paper, and glass, and learn how recycling works in your community.
- Do not use disposable food or drink containers or tools that will end up in landfills.
- Buy local when possible, which reduces the damaging effects of transporting goods and supports your community.
- When purchasing products such as napkins, toilet paper, tissue, and trash can liners, opt for those that are made with recycled content and are biodegradable or

Eric Benson

While working as a design professional, Eric Benson began educating himself about the relationship between the materials consumed in the creation of a designed artifact and their environmental impact. His graduate research at the University of Texas-Austin taught him the importance of utilizing fewer materials during the design phase. It also highlighted the need for a more holistic approach to sustainability through design by incorporating plans for waste elimination into the design process itself. Now as an assistant professor of graphic design at the University of Illinois, Benson's commitment to sustainable design led to the founding of Re-nourish.com, a free, unbiased, and independent resource for sustainable graphic design. Re-nourish provides information based on environmental science, industry best practices, and research conducted by Benson and his partners, Jess Sand and Yvette Perullo. One of the tools that Re-nourish provides is its Sustainable Graphic Design Standards, which offer verification upon meeting standards of established criteria in design considerations like the object's general purpose, life cycle impact, physical format, materials, manufacturing, finishing, distribution, and disposal.

Resources:
http://www.re-nourish.com/

recyclable. In fact, always try to purchase products that are recycled *and* recyclable.

- Use hot water only when necessary.
- Compost food scraps for use as fertilizer.
- Encourage alternatives to single-car commuting, such as public transport, walking, or biking. See if transportation incentive programs are available in your city or if your workplace subsidizes public or active transportation. If these are not options, set up a carpool.
- Replace regular light bulbs with high efficiency compact fluorescent (CFL) or light-emitting diode (LED) bulbs and dispose of used bulbs properly.
- Turn off all lights and computers when not in use, and change your settings to force your computer to go into power-saving mode when it idles.
- Set realistic, quantifiable, and achievable goals. For example, your office might commit to purchase at least 50% PCW content paper in the next year, and within two years switch completely to 100% PCW content paper.

Printing Tips

- Print only when necessary; carefully distinguish between the material you might prefer to have in print merely out of habit, and the material that is indispensable in hard copy.
- Save paper that has only been printed on one side and use for internal office printing.
- Make use of technology like PDF formatting and scanners to digitize hard copy data in an effort to minimize paper and toner consumption.
- If you must print or make copies, do so on both sides of every page and adjust your print settings to low toner or toner saver mode.

- Find out what kind of toner the printer uses and see if less toxic alternatives are available, switch to a solid ink printer, or find the most sustainable office printing solution available.
- Refill your ink cartridges rather than buying new ones, and recycle your computer equipment.
- Eliminate unnecessary negative space (such as formatting between chapters) to reduce the amount of paper used.
- Preview documents before printing to make sure you're getting what you want the first time you print, and keep print jobs on an "economy," lower-quality setting for unofficial documents.

Paper Tips

- If you work in an office environment, write a formal paper policy. Green Press Initiative and What's In Your Paper? both have excellent sample policies on their websites that can be modified to suit the priorities, needs, and constraints unique to your department.
- Coordinate with other departments to purchase paper in bulk; doing so will mean better prices and fewer delivery trucks on the road.
- When purchasing paper, select an uncoated option rather than clay-coated whenever possible.
- Use the lowest weight paper that suits the job. For every five-pound increase in basis weight, you're using roughly 10% more paper.
- Purchase only FSC-certified (or other legitimate third-party certifiers), processed chlorine-free (PCF) recycled paper. Other meaningful and important certifications are Green-e and Green Seal.
- Grays Harbor, Mohawk, Boise, Wausau, Cascades, OfficeMax, and Xerox all offer 100% recycled copy

papers. See also Conservatree's Recycled Copy Paper Listings (conservatree.com/public/localsources/copy-paper.html). Arvey Paper, the PaperZone, OfficeMax, Office Depot, and Staples stock many of these brands at competitive prices.

- If you don't see 100% recycled copy paper, ask for it. Often stores keep this in a back storeroom because it's not in high enough demand to showcase in the store, so don't assume it's not available just because it's not visible.

- Cultivating relationships with local paper suppliers will help keep you informed of the latest developments in paper technology. You can also stay updated by visiting the Green Press Initiative website.

Ink Tips

- Recycle or refill ink and toner cartridges. Consider coordinating with other departments to purchase these items.

- Become an advocate or an early adopter of soy- or vegetable-based toner for laser printers.

- When designing material for print, avoid colored inks made with heavy metals (usually metallic colors).

- Ask for mineral-free inks that are vegetable-, soy-, or water-based.

- For petroleum-based inks, use only those that contain less than 10% VOCs.

- Design for minimal ink coverage and avoid designs that bleed off the page.

Although it may cost a little more up front to make these choices, as consumer demand for sustainable supplies continues to rise, prices will continue to decrease, becoming comparable to those of regular supplies. Budgets can be restrictive, but these are reasonable goals with small, absorbable costs, especially with money saved on greater efficiency in other areas like energy consumption. According to the Green Press Initiative's report *Reducing Climate Impacts*, "almost 90% of all office energy consumption is used for lighting, heating, cooling, and ventilation, office equipment, and water heating." Clearly, reducing energy consumption can be beneficial both environmentally and economically.

The benefits of using 100% PCW content paper are impressive. The following chart displays the effects of replacing one ton of 30% PCW content paper with one ton of 100% PCW content paper, according to the Environmental Defense Fund's Paper Calculation.

Resources Saved:	Prevents the Following Emissions:
2 tons of wood 2 million BTUs total energy 6 pounds of carbon dioxide equivalent	3 pounds of nitrogen dioxide 4 pounds of particulates 3 pounds of volatile organic compounds 6,125 gallons of wastewater 787 pounds of solid waste

Many educational institutions, cities, counties, states, and an increasing number of corporations have policies addressing paper efficiency, recycling, recycled content, and cleaner production methods; some state agencies even require the use of 100% PCW content paper. When developing and implementing a paper policy, choose a starting point that's feasible. A good minimum recycled content to aim for is 30%–50%.

It can be surprising to discover how many aspects of daily life generate paper waste that extends beyond our peripheral vision, but this waste, too, should be consciously and responsibly dealt with. For example, eliminate the junk mail you receive. Sign up online with Catalog Choice, DMAchoice, or Tonic Mailstopper to change your subscription preferences with retailers, banks, and grocery stores in an effort to be as paperless as possible.

Do a little research about what your community has available; for example, the non-profit Free Geek in Portland, Oregon, accepts donations of any computer equipment, working or not. They repair and reuse the computers that they're able to, and responsibly recycle non-functioning computers and scrap. If possible, donate your equipment to an organization like Free Geek, which has signed the BAN (Basel Action Network) pledge.

Conclusion

Even the most loyal bibliophile can acknowledge that thousands of excess books are printed every year. The staunchest print enthusiast cannot deny the negative environmental impacts of the publishing industry. Romanticizing the artifact of a printed book has a certain danger, and eventually, we must draw a line at the amount of valuable, non-renewable resources we can afford to spend in book publishing. But, we must keep in mind that neither technological advances in media nor responsible printing heralds the demise of the book itself.

Given the rapidly evolving technology of e-readers and the increasingly clunky and outdated distribution system, no one knows for certain where the book industry is headed—let alone how

---

Green Press Initiative

The Green Press Initiative is a nonprofit program that works with the newspaper and book industry to reduce the ecological footprint of the publishing process. The initiative educates the industry on the conservation of natural resources, preservation of endangered forests, reduction of greenhouse gas emissions, and the minimization of various impacts on indigenous communities. The Green Press Initiative offers invaluable articles, reports, guidelines, paper and supplier listings, and sample policies. The initiative focuses on offering viable solutions to the detrimental social and environmental effects of the publishing industry. By providing these tools and encouraging publishers and printers to take steps—such as signing and implementing formal paper policies—the Green Press Initiative promotes responsible practices and informed choices. In addition to co-founding the Environmental Paper Network, it is now coordinating the Book Industry Environmental Council—a multi-stakeholder group that is establishing goals and metrics for industry expansions in environmental performance. The Green Press Initiative's Treatise on Environmentally Responsible Publishing sets measurable and attainable goals toward a more sustainable industry.

Resources:
www.greenpressinitiative.org

---

greener, more sustainable practices will manifest themselves across the industry. When comparing the complex tradeoffs of the carbon footprints between rapidly outdated electronic devices and tree-consuming books, it is impossible to examine them in isolation without considering issues of social sustainability (not everyone can afford to buy a Kindle, after all). Historically, new technology has tended to make old technology nearly obsolete. But right now nearly anyone in the United States, regardless of socio-economic position, can access printed books through their public libraries at no cost. However, if the shift toward digitization continues and if certain books exist exclusively in electronic form, we will be presented with a new set of hurdles to confront. The danger of widening the information gap between the haves and the have-nots becomes more and more obvious with expensive technology. The rate of change makes it increasingly urgent that the social sustainability of the publishing world be weighed along with issues of environmental sustainability.

The authors of this book believe that book publishing will continue to be a thriving, artful industry, but we also recognize that it is imperative for it to evolve in a more sustainable, responsible manner. While *Rethinking Paper & Ink* touches on issues of concern for the publishing industry, its authors hope that positive changes on an individual, corporate, and global level will create a silver lining for future generations. Many sustainably minded individuals and presses across the country are actively doing amazing things to improve the industry by infusing it with environmentally friendly values and practices. Significant measures can be taken at every step of the production and printing process to implement positive change. We can look to the example of leaders like Joshua Martin, Chelsea Green, and Celery Design for optimistic indicators of where sustainable publishing is heading.

Large-scale change cannot happen overnight, but it is vital that everyone continues to work toward a more responsible industry. While striving to use alternative energy options is an excellent place to start, there are more tactics that can be explored. Paper manufacturers can do their part by continuing to expand their recycled paper options, exploring better alternative fibers, and working with certification bodies to ensure that any virgin fiber is harvested sustainably. Printers can strive to offer more sustainable printing options, including paper, ink, and less wasteful printing processes. Ink manufacturers can work together to create a universal ecolabel that transparently represents their product. Distributors and booksellers can work together to better select stock so that the majority of books on the shelf sell and everyone wins. Publishers can establish a set of in-house sustainability goals and ensure that they extend to every facet of production, including choosing responsible and conscientious out-of-house manufacturers. Incorporating the triple bottom line ideology into a business model requires recognition of the economic, environmental, and social costs of traditional practices. When the true costs of our current practices are evaluated, it becomes clear that to meet the needs of future generations, the publishing industry must remember that *more sustainable* does not mean *more expensive*. It's imperative for the long-term health of the industry, the people working in it, and the planet. But don't forget that there are great possibilities when it comes to innovative, sustainable solutions.

Next time you find yourself fondly caressing the yellowed leaves of your favorite book, take a moment to think about why you are so attached to the book; consider how sustainable it might be; and, finally, think about how these notions are situated in the broader picture of an industry that is transforming the way we read.

1. The New Economics Foundation, "The Unhappy Planet Index: Why Good Lives Don't Have to Cost the Earth," http://www.happyplanetindex.org/public-data/files/happy-planet-index-2-0.pdf (accessed on August 15, 2010).

2. United Nations Development Programme, Human Development Reports, http://hdr.undp.org/en/ (accessed on August 15, 2010).

3. Wikipedia Entry, "Gini coefficient," http://en.wikipedia.org/wiki/Gini_coefficient (accessed on August 15, 2010).

4. Resiliance Alliance, "Panarchy," http://www.resalliance.org/593.php (accessed on August 14, 2010).

5. Thompson, John B, *Merchants of Culture: The Publishing Business in the Twenty-First Century*, Cambridge, MA: Polity Press, 2010, p. 72–73.

6. Green Press Initiative, "Environmental Trends and Impacts," p. 2, available from http://www.greenpressinitiative.org/orderform.htm (accessed on April 10, 2010).

7. Thompson, John B, *Merchants of Culture: The Publishing Business in the Twenty-First Century*, Cambridge, MA: Polity Press, 2010, p. 266.

8. Thompson, John B, *Merchants of Culture: The Publishing Business in the Twenty-First Century*, Cambridge, MA: Polity Press, 2010, p. 18.

9. Thompson, John B, *Merchants of Culture: The Publishing Business in the Twenty-First Century*, Cambridge, MA: Polity Press, 2010, p.

284.10. Environmental Protection Agency, "Municipal Solid Waste Generation, Recycling, and Disposal in the United States: Facts and Figures for 2008," p. 4, http://www.epa.gov/osw/nonhaz/municipal/pubs/msw2008rpt.pdf (accessed on April 10, 2010).

11. Environmental Protection Agency, "Municipal Solid Waste Generation, Recycling, and Disposal in the United States: Facts and Figures for 2008," p. 5, http://www.epa.gov/osw/nonhaz/municipal/pubs/msw2008rpt.pdf (accessed on April 10, 2010).

12. Environmental Protection Agency, "Methane," http://www.epa.gov/methane/ (accessed on April 10, 2010).

13. Green Press Initiative, "Environmental Trends and Impacts," p. 29, available from http://www.greenpressinitiative.org/orderform.htm (accessed on April 10, 2010).

14. Environmental Paper Network, "Understanding Recycled Fiber," p. 1, http://www.environmentalpaper.org/documents/recycledfiberfactsheet2.pdf (accessed on April 10, 2010).

15. Environmental Paper Network, "A Brighter Shade of Green," p. 9, http://www.environmentalpaper.org/documents/A%20Brighter%20Shade%20of%20Green%20-%20Full%20Report.pdf (accessed on April 10, 2010).

16. Green Press Initiative, "Environmental Trends and Impacts," p. 2, available from http://www.greenpressinitiative.org/orderform.htm (accessed on April 10, 2010).

17. Environmental Paper Network, "A Brighter Shade of Green," p. 9, http://www.environmentalpaper.org/documents/A%20Brighter%20Shade%20of%20Green%20-%20Full%20Report.pdf (accessed on April 10, 2010).

18. Greenpeace, "Consuming the Boreal Forest," p. 13, http://www.greenpeace.org/canada/Global/canada/report/2007/9/consuming-the-boreal-forest-t.pdf (accessed on April 10, 2010).

19. Environmental Paper Network, "A Brighter Shade of Green," p. 12, http://www.environmentalpaper.org/documents/A%20Brighter%20Shade%20of%20Green%20-%20Full%20Report.pdf (accessed on April 10, 2010).

20. Greenpeace, "Consuming the Boreal Forest," p. 19, http://www.greenpeace.org/canada/Global/canada/report/2007/9/consuming-the-boreal-forest-t.pdf (accessed on April 10, 2010).

21. Greenpeace, "Consuming the Boreal Forest," p. 4, 16, http://www.greenpeace.org/canada/Global/canada/report/2007/9/consuming-the-boreal-forest-t.pdf (accessed on April 10, 2010).

22. Environmental Paper Network, "A Brighter Shade of Green," p. 15, http://www.environmentalpaper.org/documents/A%20Brighter%20Shade%20of%20Green%20-%20Full%20Report.pdf (accessed on April 10, 2010).

23. Environmental Paper Network, "A Brighter Shade of Green," p. 5, http://www.environmentalpaper.org/documents/A%20Brighter%20Shade%20of%20Green%20-%20Full%20Report.pdf (accessed on April 10, 2010).

24. Environmental Paper Network, "A Brighter Shade of Green," p. 11, http://www.environmentalpaper.org/documents/A%20Brighter%20Shade%20of%20Green%20-%20Full%20Report.pdf (accessed on April 10, 2010).

25. Environmental Paper Network, "A Brighter Shade of Green," p. 11, http://www.environmentalpaper.org/documents/A%20

Brighter%20Shade%20of%20Green%20-%20Full%20Report.pdf (accessed on April 10, 2010).

26. Greenpeace, "Consuming the Boreal Forest," p. 16, http://www.greenpeace.org/canada/Global/canada/report/2007/9/consuming-the-boreal-forest-t.pdf (accessed on April 10, 2010).

27. Greenpeace, "Consuming the Boreal Forest," p. 4, http://www.greenpeace.org/canada/Global/canada/report/2007/9/consuming-the-boreal-forest-t.pdf (accessed on April 10, 2010).

28. Environmental Paper Network, "A Brighter Shade of Green," p. 16, http://www.environmentalpaper.org/documents/A%20Brighter%20Shade%20of%20Green%20-%20Full%20Report.pdf (accessed on April 10, 2010).

29. Green Press Initiative, "Feeling the Impacts of Paper: Indigenous to Canada, Ontario's *Grassy Narrows First Nation* Stands Up in Defense of Their Land," http://www.greenpressinitiative.org/documents/FeelingImpactsofPaper.pdf (accessed on December 14, 2010).

30. Environmental Paper Network, "The State of the Paper Industry: Monitoring the Indicators of Environmental Performance," p. 14, http://www.environmentalpaper.com/documents/StateOfPaperIndSm.pdf (accessed on April 10, 2010).

31. Food and Agriculture Organization of the United Nations, "Environmental impact assessment and environmental auditing in the pulp and paper industry," 3.2.3.5, http://www.fao.org/docrep/005/v9933e/V9933E00.htm#TOC (accessed on April 10, 2010).

32. Food and Agriculture Organization of the United Nations, "Environmental impact assessment and environmental auditing in the

pulp and paper industry," 3.2.3.5, http://www.fao.org/docrep/005/
v9933e/V9933E00.htm#TOC (accessed on April 10, 2010).

33. Steve Douglas, "So You Think You Know the Recycle Logo?"
The Logo Factory, http://www.thelogofactory.com/logo_blog/
index.php/the-recycle-logo/ (accessed December 14, 2010).

34. Environmental Defense Fund, Paper Calculator, http://www.
edf.org/papercalculator/ (accessed on April 10, 2010).

35. Environmental Paper Network, "The State of the Paper
Industry: Monitoring the Indicators of Environmental
Performance," p. 13, http://www.environmentalpaper.com/docu-
ments/StateOfPaperIndSm.pdf (accessed on April 10, 2010).

36. Environmental Paper Network, "A Brighter Shade of Green,"
p. 6, 22, http://www.environmentalpaper.org/documents/A%20
Brighter%20Shade%20of%20Green%20-%20Full%20Report.pdf
(accessed on April 10, 2010).

37. Environmental Paper Network, "A Brighter Shade of Green,"
p. 22, http://www.environmentalpaper.org/documents/A%20
Brighter%20Shade%20of%20Green%20-%20Full%20Report.pdf
(accessed on April 10, 2010).

38. Forest Stewardship Council, "FSC Principles and Criteria,"
http://www.fsc.org/pc.html (accessed on April 10, 2010).

39. Mireya Navarro, "Environmental Groups Spar Over
Certifications of Wood and Paper Products," *The New York Times*,
http://www.nytimes.com/2009/09/12/science/earth/12timber.html
(accessed December 15, 2010).

40. Environmental Paper Network, "The State of the Paper
Industry: Monitoring the Indicators of Environmental

Performance," p. 48–50, http://www.environmentalpaper.com/documents/StateOfPaperIndSm.pdf (accessed on April 10, 2010).

41. Environmental Paper Network, "The State of the Paper Industry: Monitoring the Indicators of Environmental Performance," p. 47, http://www.environmentalpaper.com/documents/StateOfPaperIndSm.pdf (accessed on April 10, 2010).

42. Michael R. Van Den Heuvel, et al., "Monitoring the Effects of Pulp and Paper Effluent is Restricted in Genetically Distinct Populations of Common Bully," *Environmental Science Technology*, 41 (2007), 2602–2608.

43. Environmental Paper Network, "The State of the Paper Industry: Monitoring the Indicators of Environmental Performance," p. 50–52, http://www.environmentalpaper.com/documents/StateOfPaperIndSm.pdf (accessed on April 10, 2010).

44. Environmental Paper Network, "The State of the Paper Industry: Monitoring the Indicators of Environmental Performance," p. 50–52, http://www.environmentalpaper.com/documents/StateOfPaperIndSm.pdf (accessed on April 10, 2010).

45. World Bank Group, "Pulp and Paper Mills," p. 398, http://www.ifc.org/ifcext/enviro.nsf/AttachmentsByTitle/gui_pulp_WB/$FILE/pulp_PPAH.pdf (accessed on April 10, 2010).

46. World Bank Group, "Pulp and Paper Mills," p. 397–98, http://www.ifc.org/ifcext/enviro.nsf/AttachmentsByTitle/gui_pulp_WB/$FILE/pulp_PPAH.pdf (accessed on April 10, 2010).

47. Environmental Protection Agency, "Control Techniques Guidelines for Offset Lithographic Printing and Letterpress Printing," p.8, http://www.epa.gov/ttncaaa1/t3/fr_notices/litho_print_ctg_092906.pdf (accessed on April 10, 2010); Wendy

Jedlicka, *Sustainable Graphic Design* (New York: Wiley, 2010), p. 343.

48. Environmental Protection Agency, "Cleaner Technologies Substitutes Assessment: Lithographic Blanket Washes," p. 1–9, http://www.epa.gov/dfe/pubs/lithography/ctsa/litho.pdf (accessed on April 10, 2010).

49. Morawsa, Lidia, et al. "Particle Emission Characteristics of Office Printers," *International Labarotory for Air Quality and Health*, pp. 1–7, http://cdn.sfgate.com/chronicle/acrobat/2007/08/01/printer_es063049z.pdf (accessed December 15, 2010).

50. Hewlett-Packard, "HP Indigo Environmental White Paper," p. 9, http://www.hp.com/hpinfo/newsroom/press_kits/2008/predrupa/wp_HpindigoEnvironmental.pdf (accessed on April 10, 2010).

51. Hewlett-Packard, "HP and the Environment," p. 3, https://h30406.www3.hp.com/campaigns/2008/events/takeaction/commercial/images/Enviroment-Brochure.pdf (accessed on April 10, 2010).

52. Hewlett-Packard, "HP's Environmental Goals and Policies," http://www.hp.com/hpinfo/globalcitizenship/environment/commitment/goals.html (accessed on April 10, 2010).

53. Environmental Protection Agency, "Control Techniques Guidelines for Offset Lithographic Printing and Letterpress Printing," p.12, http://www.epa.gov/ttncaaa1/t3/fr_notices/litho_print_ctg_092906.pdf (accessed on April 10, 2010).

54. Environmental Protection Agency, "Cleaner Technologies Substitutes Assessment: Lithographic Blanket Washes," pp. 1–10, http://www.epa.gov/dfe/pubs/lithography/ctsa/litho.pdf (accessed on April 10, 2010).

55. Environmental Protection Agency, "Printing Industry and Use Cluster Profile," p. ES-1, http://www.epa.gov/dfe/pubs/printing/cluster/part-1.pdf (accessed on April 10, 2010).

56. Greg Kozak, "Printed Scholarly Books and E-Book Reading Devices: A Comparative Lifecycle Assessment of Two Book Options," p. 30–31, http://css.snre.umich.edu/css_doc/CSS03-04.pdf (accessed on April 10, 2010).

57. Environmental Protection Agency, "Control Techniques Guidelines for Offset Lithographic Printing and Letterpress Printing," p. 7, http://www.epa.gov/ttncaaa1/t3/fr_notices/litho_print_ctg_092906.pdf (accessed on April 10, 2010).

58. Brian Dougherty, *Green Graphic Design* (New York: Allworth Press, 2008), p. 119–120.

59. Ecofont, "Save Ink and Toner with Ecofont," http://www.ecofont.com/en/products/green/printing/saving-printing-costs-and-eco-friendly/save-ink-and-toner.html (accessed on April 10, 2010).

60. Calculated with Re-Nourish's Paper Calculator: http://re-nourish.com/?l=tools_projectcalculator.

61. Calculated with Re-Nourish's Project Calculator: http://re-nourish.com/?l=tools_projectcalculator.

62. Calculated with Re-Nourish's Project Calculator: http://re-nourish.com/?l=tools_projectcalculator.

63. Bowker, "Book Industry Statistics," http://www.bowkerinfo.com/bowker/IndustryStats2010.pdf (accessed on December 15, 2010).

64. Green Press Initiative, "Environmental Trends and Impacts," p. 2, available from http://www.greenpressinitiative.org/orderform. htm (accessed on April 10, 2010).

65. Environmnetal Protection Agency, "Report to Congress on Server and Data Center Energy Efficiency," p. 7, http://www. energystar.gov/ia/partners/prod_development/downloads/EPA_ Datacenter_Report_Congress_Final1.pdf (accessed on April 10, 2010).

66. Treehugger, "What is the Envorinmental Impact of the Internet?" http://www.treehugger.com/files/2009/05/what-is-the-environmental-impact-of-the-internet.php (accessed on April 10, 2010).

67. Calculated using the EPA's Greenhouse Gas Equivalencies Calculator: http://www.epa.gov/cleanenergy/energy-resources/calculator.html.

68. Greenpeace, "Where Does E-waste End Up?" http://www. greenpeace.org/international/en/campaigns/toxics/electronics/the-e-waste-problem/where-does-e-waste-end-up/ (accessed on April 10, 2010).

69. Basel Action Network, "Exporting Harm: The High-Tech Trashing of Asia," p. 11, http://www.greenpeace.org/interna-tional/en/campaigns/toxics/electronics/the-e-waste-problem/what-s-in-electronic-devices/bfr-pvc-toxic/ (accessed on April 10, 2010).

70. Greg Kozak, "Printed Scholarly Books and E-Book Reading Devices: A Comparative Lifecycle Assessment of Two Book Options," p. 91, http://css.snre.umich.edu/css_doc/CSS03-04.pdf (accessed on April 10, 2010).

71. Martin LaMonica, "Study Paints Kindle E-reader a Dark Shade of Green," http://news.cnet.com/8301-11128_3-10320334-54.html (accessed on April 10, 2010).

72. Daniel Goleman and Gregory Norris, "How Green is My iPad?" http://www.nytimes.com/interactive/2010/04/04/opinion/04opchart.html (accessed on April 10, 2010).

73. Green Press Initiative, "Environmental Trends and Impacts," p. 8, available from http://www.greenpressinitiative.org/orderform.htm (accessed on April 10, 2010).

74. Environmental Protection Agency, "eCycling: Frequent Questions," http://www.epa.gov/epawaste/conserve/materials/ecycling/faq.htm#recycled (accessed on April 10, 2010).

75. Environmental Protection Agency, " Statistics on the Management of Used and End-of-Life Electronics," http://www.epa.gov/epawaste/conserve/materials/ecycling/manage.htm (accessed on April 10, 2010).

76. Lenovo, "Highest Amounts of Recycled Content and Enhanced VoIP Web Conferencing," http://news.lenovo.com/article_display.cfm?article_id=1338 (accessed on April 10, 2010).

77. Charlie Sorrel, "LG's Solar-Powered E-Book Reader," http://www.wired.com/gadgetlab/2009/10/lgs-solar-powered-e-book-reader/ (accessed on April 10, 2010).

78. The New York Times, "Lusty Tales and Hot Sales: Romance E-books Thrive," http://www.nytimes.com/2010/12/09/books/09romance.html?_r=1&src=me&ref=books (accessed December 15, 2010).

79. Ipsos, "Ipsos OTX MediaCT Releases Latest Results from its Longitudinal Media eXperience Study—Offering a Full View of the American Consumers' Media Experience," http://www.ipsos-na.com/news-polls/pressrelease.aspx?id=4957 (accessed on October 3, 2010).

80. Darcy Hitchcock and Marsha Willard, *The Business Guide to Sustainability: Practical Strategies and Tools for Organizations* (London: Earthscan Ltd., 2006), p. 181.

Glossary

abiotic environment | An environment that is unable to sustain life due to a lack of oxygen, food sources, or other necessary elements. These can be created through toxic emissions released into previously livable environments.

aerobic disintegration | A natural decomposition process that requires the presence of oxygen.

alternative fibers | Non-wood materials for making papers, including hemp, kenaf, bamboo, banana leaves, and agricultural residues such as grass clippings.

anaerobic processes | A biological or chemical process that can take place in the absence of oxygen.

aqueous coating | A type of protective paper coating that is water-based instead of petroleum-based. This coating is environmentally preferable to coatings such as laminates or varnishes as it releases significantly fewer vocs during the application and drying processes.

backlit display | Electronic visual displays that require backlighting and, therefore, the use of more energy. These include screens lit by LCD (liquid crystal displays) and by LED (light-emitting diodes).

best practices | The processes, practices, and systems that allow for the most desirable outcome for a given industry.

biochemical oxygen demand (BOD) | A measurement of the effectiveness of water emission reduction programs. The figure is determined by measuring the amount of oxygen needed by aerobic biological organisms to break down any organic pollutants present in a water sample.

biodiversity | The concept of measuring the health of an ecosystem by considering the amount of variable life forms within it. A significant negative factor, which affects a system's biodiversity, is extinction of a species through direct removal (i.e., clear-cutting a specific species of tree for wood fiber) or indirect removal (i.e., removing an animal's necessary food source).

biological magnification | The increasing accumulation of a compound, such as mercury or arsenic, as it moves up the food chain.

biomass | Biological material from living or recently living organisms, specifically referring to trees removed from forests for paper production. When incinerated, biomass waste is capable of producing enough heat to be a potential alternative energy source.

black liquor | A byproduct of kraft pulping composed of lignin residues, hemicelluloses, and the inorganic chemicals used to extract individual paper fibers from the pulp mixture. Black liquor can be burned in recovery boilers as an alternative source of energy.

BLAD (basic layout and design) | A sample of a book's interior design, used for marketing purposes.

bleed | A printing term for ink that extends beyond the margins to the edge of the page.

brominated flame retardants (BFRs) | A bromine-based polymer applied to electronic products to reduce their flammability. These compounds are lipophilic and bioaccumulative, meaning they accumulate and are stored in the fat cells of humans and other animals. Their toxicity can cause negative effects in digestive, endocrine, and nervous systems.

built-in obsolescence | The idea that technological devices are not manufactured to be long-lasting with the objective being that the consumer will purchase a newer device upon its release.

by-product | A secondary or incidental product produced by a process that is not the primary product or service being produced.

calendering | A finishing process in which paper is passed through pressurized heated rollers to impose a certain finish to give it a smooth or textured feel.

CAMALS | An acronym for the following group of highly toxic heavy metals: cadmium, arsenic, mercury, antimony, lead, and selenium.

carbon dioxide (CO_2) | A gas that is released from the combustion of organic matter. It can occur naturally through the carbon cycle or through man-made emissions, such as burning fossil fuels. Carbon dioxide emissions are the most commonly measured greenhouse gas emissions and are typically associated with climate change.

carbon footprint | A measure of the environmental impact, usually through tracking greenhouse gas emissions, of a given group, project, or individual.

carbon offsets | A system by which an individual or an organization can compensate for their own carbon emissions by investing in energy alternatives, including wind power, hydroelectric energy, or other greenhouse gas reduction strategies.

carbon sequestration | A term which describes the process of removing carbon dioxide from the atmosphere. Carbon sequestration can occur artificially or naturally, through biological, chemical, and physical processes. Photosynthesis is an example of a natural biochemical process of carbon sequestration.

chain of custody (COC) | A type of certification that ensures a product has been sourced and manufactured sustainably on its way from the original source (i.e., a forest harvested for paper for books) to its end destination (i.e., the consumer who purchases the book in the bookstore). Printers, distributors, and publishers can gain COC certifications to reflect and legitimize their sustainability initiatives.

chemical oxygen demand (COD) | A measurement of the amount of oxidizable compounds—those composed of carbon and hydrogen—present in water. It can be used to determine the efficacy of effluent treatment programs.

chemical pulping | A pulping method in which wood fibers are separated through chemical processing, typically using caustic soda, sodium sulfide, sodium hydroxide, and/or chlorine compounds. This type of process provides the benefit of preserving more intact fibers and using less energy than mechanical pulping, but it produces less overall usable material for papermaking.

chlorine | A toxic gas that causes respiratory irritation. At high inhalation rates, it can react with water-containing cells in the body to produce traces of hydrochloric acid.

Clean Air Act | A federal law enacted in 1963 (and expanded in 1970) by the United States Congress to control air pollution on a national level according to guidelines developed by the Environmental Protection Agency. Amendments in 1990 further addressed issues regarding pollution related to ozone depletion and acid rain.

closed-loop | A term referring to a process that sustains itself.

CMYK | An acronym for full-color printing that encompasses the four inks that can be mixed to produce a seemingly endless spectrum of colors: cyan, magenta, yellow, and black.

coated paper | Paper that has been treated with stabilizers like chalk or china clay to provide smoothness and gloss for books that demand high-quality image reproduction, such as art or photography books. Coated paper is a less than desirable choice in terms of sustainability since these stabilizers cannot be stripped before the paper is recycled and may lead to an undesirable outcome in paper stocks produced from its recycled pulp.

cradle to cradle (C2C) | An approach in design. Rather than designing an object from the cradle to grave approach (that is, for a single use), designing it with recycling or reuse in mind, so that the quality of the material can withstand a large or indefinite number of recycling processes. The sustainability of an object or process starts with the design.

de-inking | The process of removing inks from post- and pre-consumer waste during the paper recycling process through the use of chemical surfactants.

dedicated device | A technological device manufactured to perform one specific function (e.g., a telephone or clock) as opposed to a multitasking device capable of many functions (e.g., a computer).

digital distribution | The process by which a consumer purchases and downloads a digital book, most often via the internet and an e-reader or other reading device.

digital short-run printing | A printing system distinct from offset printing, digital presses print directly from a digital file and are most often used for smaller print jobs.

digital rights management (DRM) | An access control technology that limits the use and/or sharing of digital content, like e-books and digital music files. DRM is often a controversial topic since it has both benefits (such as the prevention of piracy) and downfalls (preventing a legal owner from accessing previously purchased content on a newer device).

dioxins | A general name for a large group of toxic and highly carcinogenic chemical compounds with similar structure. These compounds are made up of carbon, oxygen, hydrogen, and chlorine atoms.

distributor | Stocks and actively sells books through sales reps to book buyers; most often they stock titles on consignment. Some venues, such as libraries, generally prefer to work with a distributor.

e-book | A digital counterpart to the printed book. This refers only to the file itself and does not include the device (i.e., an e-reader or computer) necessary to read its content.

e-ink displays | A type of screen display common in dedicated e-readers. These screens are not backlit and reduce the amount of eyestrain commonly associated with reading from computer screens for long periods of time. Their slow refresh rate makes them unsuitable for all technological devices, such as those capable of web browsing, but is appropriate for reading e-books and other simple, text-based documents.

e-waste | A term that describes discarded electronic equipment. This waste usually contains toxic materials, including polyvinyl chloride (PVC) and heavy metals like lead and mercury. If not appropriated for proper reuse or recycling, North American e-waste is commonly exported to landfills in developing nations in Asia and Africa. This causes concern for social sustainability issues in those areas.

ecolabels | Labels and logos acquired from certification organizations (such as the FSC or SFI) to signify a product's reduced environmental impact or environmental benefits.

ecosystem services | The products and services provided by eco-systems that benefit humans and are necessary for a healthy planet. Examples include: food, water, timber, carbon sequestration, oxygen production, water purification, pollination, and nutrient cycling, as well as recreational, aesthetic, and spiritual benefits.

effluent | A general term for liquid industrial waste discharge.

electrostatic precipitators | These are devices that use the principles of magnetism to charge airborne particles and draw them out of the air.

elemental chlorine-free (ECF) | Since the use of elemental chlorine in the paper-bleaching process was discontinued in the United States following an EPA ruling in 2001, many companies now use an ECF process involving chlorine dioxide, a compound said to produce less harmful waste than that produced by using pure chlorine. However, the toxic compounds and dioxins in the waste are not eliminated entirely. ECF paper, while produced to better standards than paper produced using elemental chlorine, is still less desirable from an environmental standpoint than paper processed chlorine-free (PCF) or totally chlorine-free (TCF).

extended producer responsibility (EPR) | A concept that requires owners to accept physical and financial responsibility for the impacts of their products throughout the product's entire life-cycle.

externality | The consequences and impacts of production which are not directly reflected in the price paid by the consumer.

fountain solutions | A water-based solution used during offset lithographic printing to prevent non-image areas from accepting ink. These solutions are a large component of a printer's wastewater emissions.

French folds | Two folds at right angles to one another. On a book cover, these are the front and back flaps that, when unfolded, extend beyond the trimmed book block.

furans | A type of dioxin. Observation shows that these chemical compounds are highly toxic and carcinogenic.

galleys | Promotional copies of a book's manuscript used for marketing and reviewing purposes. At this point, the manuscript has typically undergone some editing and typesetting, but is not yet finalized for full print production.

genetically modified organisms (GMOs) | Any living organism that has been altered on a molecular level that can disturb the natural evolution of biological processes.

Gini coefficient | Developed in 1912, this measurement is used in sustainability to determine social inequalities such as income distribution. The Gini coefficient is a value ranging from 0 (total equality of distribution) to 1 (total inequality of distribution).

greenhouse gases (GHG) | Gases in the Earth's atmosphere that are linked to global warming as they trap in the heat from the sun by absorption and emission of radiation. GHGs include carbon dioxide, ozone, methane, nitrous oxide, and water vapor.

Gross Domestic Product (GDP) | This is, and has been, the primary measurement of economic growth, which has become synonymous with the degree of an economy's success. It represents the total market value of all final goods and services produced in a country in a given year. GDP is equal to the total consumer, investment, and government spending plus the value of exports minus the value of imports. The basic assumption here is that an ever-growing economy is a healthy economy. There are two major problems with GDP, as far as sustainable development goes: 1) The marketplace does not properly value (or in some cases, value at all) the externalities associated with "all final goods and services," which means that the value amount used is a misrepresentation; and, 2) The expectation of an ever-growing economy (especially one that is misrepresentative) is simply not sustainable for indefinite future generations. At some point, one of those generations will have to pay the debt—most likely in the form of adegraded or depleted environment—of all the externalities we have been ignoring. This is known as inter-generational social inequity. And as long as we are measuring our economic health with measurements like GDP, we are creating social inequity.

greenwashing | A term used to describe the act of misleading consumers regarding the environmental practices of a company or the environmental benefits of a product or service.

Happy Planet Index (HPI) | Created by the New Economics Foundation (NEF) in 2006, this is a response to indices such as gdp and hdi, which do not take sustainability into account. The basic assumption of the hpi is that socio-economic growth should reflect the goal of an achievable level of happiness and health for the most people, and that the environmental costs of pursuing those goals are taken into account.

Hazardous air pollutants (HAPS) | This is a collective name for air pollutants named and regulated under Section 112 of the Clean Air Act. These pollutants are known environmental hazards.

heatsetting | Any ink drying process that involves the use of heat. Heatsetting not only requires more energy resources to power heating elements but also releases more VOCs when an ink's solution evaporates.

high conservation value forests (HCVFs) | Forests that contain significant ecological values, such as high biodiversity, endangered ecosystems, or social values that are critical to a community's liveli-hood or their spiritual or cultural identity.

human capital | This refers to the stock of talents, knowledge, and capabilities that individuals contribute to the process of the produc-tion of goods and services.

Human Development Index (HDI) | A measurement created in 1990 to address the false presumption of the GDP: that national economic growth is synonymous with human welfare. Economist Amartya Sen's work provided much of the conceptual foundation for the HDI. One of the basic concepts of this measurement is that human development is defined as a process of expanding people's choices and enhancing human capabilities and freedoms. So, things like social progress (access to education and health services), equity, participation and freedom, and human security are measured along with economic growth (GDP). Environmental costs, however, are not factored into the HDI.

indicator species | A species so closely associated with an ecosys-tem that its presence or absence is indicative of the health of that ecosystem.

inkjet | An ink distribution system found in some digital short-run printing equipment and desktop printers. In this process, liquid ink is sprayed directly onto paper. Depending on the system, the inks used in this process can be either water- or oil-based or can be UV curable.

interdependence | The dynamic relationships between all living things and the systems in which those things exist; these are rela-tionships of mutual dependence for the success or survival of each individual constituent and of the whole unit.

laminates | A petroleum-based coating, typically composed of nylon, polyester, or polypropylene, that renders paper non-recyclable.

life cycle analysis (LCA) | A measurement of a product's environmental impact throughout its usable life, from manufacturing through disposal.

lignin | A naturally occurring chemical compound found in wood fiber. The presence of lignin in paper weakens it and causes it to yellow over time.

make-ready | Paper consumed during the calibration of an offset printing press. It often represents up to 10% of paper used in a print run. It is sometimes referred to as "broke."

marketing collateral | The collection of media used to promote a book that traditionally includes bookmarks, posters, and postcards, among other items.

material safety data sheet (MSDS) | A form that describes the properties and hazards of a given chemical substance.

mechanical binding | A method in which pages are bound by mechanical means, often with spirals, posts, or staples (also called saddle-stitching), instead of using chemical adhesives that release VOCs. Mechanically bound books are easier to recycle since the binding implements can be fully filtered out before repulping.

mechanical pulping | A pulping process in which wood is physically ground into pulp for papermaking. It is more efficient than chemical pulping, but is also more energy intensive. Fiber that has been processed through mechanical pulping is typically weaker than its chemically processed counterpart due to the presence of broken fibers and lignin.

methane | A potent greenhouse gas that degrades the ozone layer and is twenty times more effective at trapping heat within the Earth's atmosphere than carbon dioxide.

multitasking device | An electronic device (e.g., a computer or smartphone) that is capable of performing many different functions, including (but not limited to) reading e-book files, web browsing, and word processing.

nitrogen dioxide | A toxic gas that is reddish-brown and has a sharp odor. This prominent air pollutant can cause acid rain and contributes to the formation of tropospheric ozone.

offset lithography | A printing process in which images are offset onto another surface before being printed on a paper surface. Many larger printing projects are done by offset printing.

old-growth forests | Sometimes referred to as intact or natural forests, old-growth forests have not been disturbed by deforestation. Trees in old-growth forests can range in age from 150–500 years.

ozone | In the Earth's upper atmosphere, ozone filters harmful UV light and prevents it from reaching the planet's surface. However, when it remains close to the surface, it is a pollutant that can cause lung irritation and respiratory problems in humans and can damage certain plants.

panarchy | The concept that ecosystems and social-ecosystems exist in hierarchies of cycles that adapt to changes. According to the theory of panarchy, the more diversity a system has, the more resilience it has—the more resilience a system has, the more able it is to adapt to changes. The ability to adapt to changes is what allows a system to be sustained.

particulate matter | Microscopic solids or liquids suspended in gas or liquid. Inhalation can cause lung cancer, asthma, or cardiovascular issues.

perfect binding | A common binding method for paperback books. Pages, within a heavier paper cover, are bound by an adhesive applied to the book's spine.

plantations | A forest that has been replanted by logging companies after the removal of old-growth. Plantations usually consist of a single species, eliminating the original forest's biodiversity. Plantations also cannot repair interrupted terrestrial carbon sequestration or make up for emissions released by logging machinery.

polyvinyl chloride (PVC) | A chlorinated plastic that was once common in the manufacturing process of electronic devices. Vinyl chloride monomer (VCM)—a basic component of pvc—is highly toxic, carcinogenic, and even explosive. When incinerated, PVC releases dioxins into the surrounding atmosphere.

print on demand (POD) | A type of distribution in which books are quickly printed and shipped after they have been ordered.

processed chlorine-free (PCF) | PCF paper must contain at least 30% post-consumer waste, for which no chlorine was used in the recycling process. It may also contain virgin paper, but that content must be produced totally chlorine-free (TCF). pcf paper may contain chlorine in the post-consumer fiber; however, that chlorine comes from the bleaching process that was originally used in the recovered paper, but not from the subsequent recycling process.

post-consumer waste (PCW) | Paper recovered from consumers and recycled into new paper.

pre-consumer fiber | Fiber, recovered from mills and production processes, that was never incorporated into a product that reached a consumer.

recovery boilers | Special tanks present in pulping mills and paper manufacturing facilities that burn waste to provide heat for energy. Their use puts less of a strain on non-renewable energy resources and also reduces solid waste emissions.

remaindered book | A book that is not selling. A publisher sells it on a nonreturnable basis at a large discount. The publisher takes a loss on each copy sold as a remainder, but recovers a little of the initial investment and clears space in the warehouse. The overproduction of books and unpredictability, or overestimation, of sales greatly increases a book's chance of becoming a remainder.

resin | A sticky plant secretion commonly found in coniferous trees. Resins are removed from wood fiber during pulping processes. Resins can be used as bio-derived additives in inks and adhesives.

royalties | Payment from the publisher to the author, typically agreed upon as a percentage of revenues based on the book's sales.

sales representatives | Rather than selling books directly to consumers, sales representatives deal with other booksellers and may specialize in certain types of books. They generally stay abreast of new books and trends, and the changing interests of readers and personally market the books to potential buyers.

self-auditing | A process in which a company outlines the environmental impact of its product or service in order to provide transparency to its methods. This can be used alongside third-party certifications in order to avoid greenwashing.

signature | A section of book pages gathered together after folding and cutting; multiple signatures are then gathered together and bound. Common page counts in one signature are sixteen or thirty-two.

slush pile | Publishing jargon for unsolicited manuscripts, notably named after the very waste that comes from paper mills.

sodium hydroxide | A chemical compound that is a caustic base. This compound is also known as lye or caustic soda.

sodium sulfide | A colorless salt that produces alkaline solutions. This compound reacts with moist air to produce the familiar rotten air odor associated with sulfur.

spot processes | In book design, a specifically mixed color that often corresponds to a color cataloging system. Choosing a spot process only requires one ink while printing the same color with CMYK variables requires four.

subsidiary rights | Rights that are subsidiary, or secondary, to the right of publishing the literary work in book form. These rights include electronic rights, movie and television rights, audio book rights, audiovisual rights, merchandizing rights, and dramatic or performance rights.

substrate | Any material that receives ink in the printing process. In book printing, the most common substrate is paper.

sulfur dioxide (SO_2) | A chemical compound that can cause environmental problems, such as acid rain, when present in emissions.

surfactant | A chemical compound that lowers the surface tension of a liquid. In recycling processes, surfactants free the pigment particles of ink from the paper, allowing them to be collected separately in the form of sludge.

tall oil | Also referred to as liquid rosin, tall oil can be distilled from black liquor—a byproduct of the kraft pulping process. This substance can be repurposed as a component of inks and adhesives.

terrestrial biospheric carbon | The carbon dioxide (CO_2) that is naturally stored by existing biomass.

totally chlorine-free (TCF) | This grade refers to virgin paper that uses no chlorine or chlorine compounds in the bleaching process. tcf is only applicable to virgin fiber paper. PCF is applicable to recycled paper.

totally effluent-free | A closed loop waste system for manufacturing mills. By limiting use of harmful compounds and reusing wastewater within the facility, plants can avoid releasing toxic effluent into local water supplies.

toner | A carbon-polymer powder used in place of ink in laser printers and copiers; it is fused to the paper with heat.

tree-free | A designation for paper made from alternative fibers, often grown agriculturally, such as hemp, cotton, or kenaf.

trim size | A book's final size after the excess edges have been removed and production is complete. Common trim sizes for trade books in the U.S. include 5.5"×8.5", 6"×9", 8.5"×11".

triple bottom line | A method of measuring overall performance based on the economic, environmental, and social performances of a business, rather than the traditional single bottom line approach, which only considers economic factors.

uncoated paper | Unlike coated paper, uncoated paper does not receive additional chemical treatment after it has been formed into sheets. It is typically a more desirable alternative as it provides purer fiber when recycled.

upcycling | Closely related to the cradle to cradle theory, this is the idea of recycling a product into one that is longer lasting or more usable than it was originally. This is opposed to downcycling, in which the new product is degraded in order to be reused.

UV coatings | Paper coatings that are cured through ultraviolet exposure instead of a heatset method.

ultraviolet (UV) printing | A printing process in which inks are cured through ultraviolet exposure instead of heatsetting. Because UV curing is instant, it produces significantly less VOC emissions than traditional heatset methods.

varnish | A paper coating that is essentially unpigmented ink. The coating process adds to a print run's VOC emissions. The varnish can be difficult to remove during recycling.

vegetable-based ink | Ink produced with a vegetable-oil base. This ink is an environmentally conscious alternative to petroleum-based inks.

virgin fiber | Material used to make paper; it comes directly from the tree and contains no recycled material.

volatile organic compounds (VOCs) | VOCs, commonly found in petroleum-based inks, are carbon-based substances that instantly vaporize at normal temperatures. They have negative effects on both the environment (they react with the nitrous oxide in the air to form ozone) and human health (they contain known carcinogens).

water-miscible | A substance that is able to mix with water in any proportion to form a completely homogenous, or uniform, solution.

waterless offset printing | An offset lithographic printing process that eliminates the water or dampening system used in conventional printing through special silicone plates, reducing wastewater and VOC emissions. Because this process does not rely on fountain solutions to transfer the ink to paper, less calibration is needed for each print run, which reduces make-ready waste.

wholesaler | Essentially a warehouse to store books for publishers after they are printed and awaiting distribution. Wholesalers, unlike distributors, do not market or sell books for a publisher.

Acronym Glossary

AFF | Ancient Forest Friendly
BAN | Basel Action Network
BFR | brominated flame retardant
BIEC | Book Industry Environmental Council
BLAD | basic layout and design
BOD | biochemical oxygen demand
BRC | bio-derived renewable content
BTU | British thermal unit
C2C | cradle to cradle
CAA | Clean Air Act
CAMALS | cadmium, arsenic, mercury, antimony, lead, selenium
CFL. | compact fluorescent light
CLMP | Council of Literary Magazines and Presses
CMYK | cyan, magenta, yellow, black
CO2 | carbon dioxide
COC | chain of custody
COD | chemical oxygen demand
DRM | digital rights management
ECF | elemental chlorine-free
EDF | Environmental Defense Fund
EPA | Environmental Protection Agency
EPR | Extended Producer Responsibility
EVA | ethylene vinyl acetate
F&G | folded & gathered (sheets)
FM | forest management
FSC | Forest Stewardship Council
GDP | gross domestic product
GHG | greenhouse gas
GMO | genetically modified organism
GPI | Green Press Initiative
HAP | hazardous air pollutant
HDI | human development index

HPI | happy planet index
HCVF | high conservation value forest
LED | light-emitting diode
LCA | life cycle analysis
LCD | liquid crystal display
MSDS | material safety data sheet
NGO | non-governmental organization
PCF | processed chlorine-free
PCW | post-consumer waste
PEFC | Programme for the Endorsment of Forest Certification
POD | print on demand
PUR | polyurethane
PVA | polyvinyl acetate
PVC | polyvinyl chloride
RA | Rainforest Alliance
SARD | severe airway restrictive disorder
SFI | Sustainable Forestry Initiative
TCF | totally chlorine-free
TEF | totally effluent-free
UV | ultraviolet
VOC | volatile organic compound

References

Bann, David. *The All New Print Production Handbook*. New York: Watson-Guptill Publications, 2006.

Bringhurst, Robert. *The Elements of Typographic Style*. Points Robert, WA: Hartley & Marks, 2005.

Dougherty, Brian. *Green Graphic Design*. New York: Allworth Press, 2008.

Elkington, John. *Cannibals with Forks: The Triple Bottom Line of 21ˢᵗ Century Business*. London: Capstone Publishing, 1997.

Epstein, Jason. *Book Business: Publishing Past, Present, and Future*. New York: W.W. Norton, 2001.

Evans, Poppy. *Forms, Folds, and Sizes*. Gloucester, MA: Rockport Publishers, 2004.

Grant, John. *The Green Marketing Manifesto*. New York: Wiley, 2008.

Gunderson, Lance H. and C. S. Holling, Editors. *Panarchy: Understanding Transformations in Systems of Humans and Nature*. Washington D. C.: Island Press, 2001.

Haslam, Andrew. *Book Design*. New York: Abrams, 2006.

Hitchcock, Darcy and Marsha Willard. *The Business Guide to Sustainability: Practical Strategies and Tools for Organizations*. London: Earthscan Ltd., 2006.

Jedlicka, Wendy. *Sustainable Graphic Design*. New York: Wiley, 2010.

Kaplan, Jennifer. *Greening Your Small Business: How to Improve Your Bottom Line, Grow Your Brand, Satisfy Your Customers—and Save the Planet*. New York: Prentice Hall Press, 2009.

McDonough, William and Michael Braungart. *Cradle to Cradle: Remaking the Way We Make Things*. New York: North Point Press, 2002.

Sherin, Aaris. *SustainAble: a Handbook of Materials and Applications for Graphic Designers and Their Clients*. Beverly, MA: Rockport Publishers, 2008.

Schiffrin, Andre. *The Business of Books*. 2000. Reprint. London: Verso Books, 2001.

Thompson, John B. *Merchants of Culture: The Publishing Business in the Twenty-First Century*. Cambridge, MA: Polity Press, 2010.

Resources

Shipping & Distribution

Chelsea Green's Green Partners Program
www.chelseagreen.com
Sustainable Packaging Coalition
www.sustainablepackaging.org

Print Production

Paper
Chlorine Free Products Association
www.chlorinefreeproducts.org
Conservatree
www.conservatree.com
Environmental Defense Fund Paper Calculator
www.edf.org/papercalculator
Environmental Paper Network
www.environmentalpaper.org
ForestEthics
www.forestethics.org
Metafore
www.metafore.org
Melcher Media
www.melchermedia.com
Natural Resources Defense Council
www.nrdc.org
Paper Specs
www.paperspecs.com
What's in Your Paper?
www.whatsinyourpaper.com

Paper Manufacturers and Distributors

Boise Paper
www.boiseinc.com
Cascades
www.cascades.com
Grays Harbor Paper
www.ghplp.com
Living Tree Paper
www.livingtreepaper.com
Neenah Paper
www.neenahpaper.com
New Leaf Paper
www.newleafpaper.com
Mohawk Fine Papers
www.mohawkpaper.com
Spicers Paper
www.spicerspaper.com
Wausau Paper
www.wausaupaper.com

Ink

American Soybean Association's SoySeal
www.soygrowers.com/resources/soyink.htm
The National Association of Printing Ink Manufacturers (NAPIM)
www.napim.org
Pantone
www.pantone.com
Sun Chemical
www.sunchemical.com

Printing

Hemlock Printers
www.hemlock.com
Maple-Vail Book Manufacturing Group
www.maple-vail.com

Pinball Publishing
www.pinballpublishing.com
Printer's National Environmental Assistance Center
www.pneac.org
Sustainable Green Printing Partnership
www.sgppartnership.org
Thomson-Shore
www.thomsonshore.com
Waterless Printing Association
www.waterless.org

Certification Programs
Forest Stewardship Council
www.fscus.org
Green-e
www.green-e.org
Green Seal
www.greenseal.org
Programme for the Endorsement of Forest Certification schemes
(PEFC)
www.pefc.org
Sustainable Forestry Initiative (SFI)
www.sfiprogram.org

Pre-Press
Catalog Choice
www.catalogchoice.org
Council of Literary Magazines and Presses
www.clmp.org
DMAchoice
www.dmachoice.org
Submissions Manager
www.submissionmanager.net

Sustainable Design

Celery Design Collaborative
www.celerydesign.com

Design by Nature
www.designbynature.org

GreenBlue
www.greenblue.org

The Living Principles
www.livingprinciples.org

O_2 Global Network
www.o2.org

Organic Design Operatives (ODO)
www.themightyodo.com

Re-nourish
www.re-nourish.com

Electronics

Basel Action Network
www.ban.org

Cleantech
www.cleantech.com

Free Geek
www.freegeek.org

Hewlett-Packard
www.hp.com

Marketing

Booksquare
www.booksquare.com

Sustainability Issues

The Book Industry Environmental Council (BIEC)
www.bookcouncil.org

Canopy
www.canopyplanet.org
Earth Policy Institute
www.earthpolicy.org
Eco-libris
www.ecolibris.net
Environmental Defense Fund
www.edf.org
Food and Agriculture Organization of the United Nations
www.fao.org
Grassroots Recycling Network
www.grrn.org
Greenpeace
www.greenpeace.org
Green Press Initiative
www.greenpressinitiative.org
Rainforest Alliance
www.rainforest-alliance.org
Sustainable Is Good
www.sustainableisgood.com
Sustainablog
www.sustainablog.org
Treehugger
www.treehugger.com
U.S. Environmental Protection Agency
www.epa.gov

Index

C

electrostatic precipitators: 122

elemental chlorine-free (ECF) paper: 34, 122, 134

emissions: 42, 45, 49, 58, 73. *See also* greenhouse gas:

    and sulfur dioxide, 130

    carbon emissions, 16, 72

    from electronics, 72, 73, 83, 84

    from ink, 53, 54, 68

    from landfill, 20

    from paper mills, 32

    from transit, 20, 54, 69

    from wastewater, 49, 122

    volatile organic compound (VOC), 42, 49, 53, 54, 132, 135

environment: 5, 7, 8, 9, 10, 15, 16, 20, 23, 25, 27, 32, 37, 38, 39, 40, 41, 42, 43, 48, 51, 52, 54, 55, 59, 62, 63, 65, 66, 68, 71, 72, 73, 74, 75, 80, 82, 84, 87, 88, 89, 91, 95, 96, 102, 103, 104, 108, 113, 118, 121, 122, 124, 126, 129, 130, 131. *See also* ecology

    abiotic, 44

Environmental Defense Fund: 94, 100, 109, 134, 137, 141

Environmental Paper Network: 43, 102, 106, 107, 108, 109, 110, 137

Environmental Protection Agency: 45, 82, 106, 110, 111, 112, 114, 119, 134, 141

EPA: 45, 82, 106, 110, 111, 112, 114, 119, 134, 141

EPR: 83, 122, 134

e-reader: 71, 72, 73, 74, 75, 76, 77, 78, 79, 81, 83, 85, 120, 121

e-reading device:. *See* e-reader

e-Stewardship Initiative: 82

e-Stewards Program: 82

ethylene vinyl acetate (EVA): 57, 134

EVA: 57, 134

e-waste 51, 73, 74, 81, 82, 83, 113, 121

extended producer responsibility: 83, 122, 134

externality: 122

F

F&G signatures: 57, 134

FM: 38, 40, 41, 134

folded and gathered (F&G) signatures: 57, 134

Food and Agriculture Organization of the United Nations: 108, 141

forest: 16, 26, 38, 39, 40, 41, 51, 93, 107, 108, 109, 134, 135, 139. *See also* deforestation; *See also* habitat

ForestEthics: 40, 137

forest management (FM) certifications: 38, 40, 41, 134

Forest Stewardship Council (FSC): 38, 39, 40, 41, 51, 52, 89, 98, 109, 121, 134

H

I

M

N

petroleum-based ink: 54, 132
Pinball Publishing: 89, 139
plantations: 26, 128
POD: 21, 120, 128, 135
pollution: 36
polyurethane (PUR): 57, 135
polyvinyl acetate (PVA): 57, 135
polyvinyl chloride (PVC): 74, 128. *See also* e-waste
post binding: 58
post-consumer waste (PCW): 31, 97, 100, 128. *See also* PCW
pre-consumer fiber: 32, 128
pre-consumer waste: 32
press kit: 88
press release: 90
press sheet: 46
print cartridges: 48
printers: 45, 50, 66, 94. *See also* offset lithography; *See also* offset printing; *See also* printing press; *See also* print on demand; *See also* waterless offset printing
    organizations for, 138
    tips for, 94
Printer's National Environmental Assistance Center: 139
printing: 46, 89, 94, 97, 119. *See also* Ecofont; *See also* pinball publishing; *See also* Pinball Publishing; *See also* print on demand; *See also* printing press
printing press: 46
    offset, 68
    sheet fed, 46
    web-fed, 46
Print on Demand (POD): 21, 120, 128
processed chlorine-free (PCF) certification: 34, 98, 122, 128
Programme for the Endorsement of Forest Certification (PEFC): 41
public libraries:. *See* libraries
pulp: 17, 28, 33, 42, 57, 126, 129
PUR 135
PUR: 57
PVA: 57, 135
PVC: 74, 135. *See also* e-waste

R

RA: 41, 135
Rainforest Alliance (RA): 41, 141
rate of growth: 9

S

About the Author

This book is a collaborative effort made by Jessicah Carver, Natalie Guidry, and the graduate students in the publishing program at Portland State University. It is an expanded version of a booklet published under the same name by Melissa Brumer and Janine Eckhart, founders of Ooligan Press's sustainable publishing initiative. In 2009, the booklet launched Ooligan Press's line of sustainably produced books known as the OpenBook series.

Ooligan Press

Ooligan Press takes its name from a Native American word for the common smelt or candlefish. Ooligan is a general trade press rooted in the rich literary community of the Pacific Northwest and located in the Department of English at Portland State University. Ooligan is staffed by students pursuing master's degrees in an apprentice-ship program under the guidance of a core faculty of publishing professionals.

Authors:
Jessicah Carver
Natalie Guidry

**Authors of Rethinking
Paper & Ink booklet:**
Melissa Brumer
Janine Eckhart

Publishers:
Abbey Gaterud
Bradi Grebien-Samkow
Dennis Stovall

Project Managers:
Alyson Hoffman
Molly Woods

Managing Editors:
Julie Flanagan
Kenny Hanour
Netanis Waters

Developmental Writers:
Katelyn Benz
Kjerstin Johnson

Editors:
Michelle Blair
Melissa Brumer
Mary Darcy
Jason Davis
Julie Flanagan
Leah Gibson-Blackfeather
Amanda Gomm
Taylor Hudson
Kjerstin Johnson
Shawnell Johnson
Rachel Moore
Kate Savage
Lucy Softich
Susan Wiget
Cheri Woods-Edwin

Indexer:
Susan E. Wiget

Proofers:
Kathryn Banks
Katelyn Benz
Leah Brown
Leah Gibson-Blackfeather
Stephanie Kroll
Amanda Winterroth

Marketing Managers:
Cooper Lee Bombardier
Candice Peaslee

Marketing Team:
Michelle Blair
Bryan Coffelt
Noel Conrad
Jody Gastoni
Laura Gleim
Kristin Howe
Cory Mimms
Shawnell Johnson
Kelsey Klockenteger
Anne Paulsen
Anne Peasley
Chelsea Pfund
Ashley Rogers
Sara Simmonds
Tracy Turpen
Missy Ward
Elisabeth Wilson
Amanda Winterroth

Cover Design:
Brian David Smith

Interior Designers:
Kerri Higby
Brian David Smith

Digital:
Sarah Schmalzer
Stefani Varney

Production Assistance:
Eliza Lane
Elisabeth Wilson

Colophon

The text of this book is set in Bembo. Cut in 1929 under the direction of Stanley Morison for the Monotype Corporation, Bembo is a revival of a humanist typeface cut by Francesco Griffo around 1495. Griffo's typeface, cut for the Venetian press of Aldus Manutius, was first used in 1496 to set a book entitled *Petri Bembi de Aetna Angelum Chalabrilem liber*, written by the Italian poet Pietro Bembo. Bembo is a relatively light-weight typeface, so it requires less leading than heavier faces. It is therefore more economical both in ink usage and page space.

The headers and industry profiles are set in Century Gothic, a typeface designed in 1991 for Monotype Imaging. Inspired by Twentieth Century (drawn between 1937 and 1947 by Sol Hess for the Lanston Monotype Company) and sharing many characteristics with the International Typeface Corporation's Avant Garde (Herb Lubalin, 1970), Century Gothic is a geometric sans serif, a style popularized in the 1920s and '30s. In 2010 the University of Wisconsin switched their standard email typeface from Arial to Century Gothic, claiming that it saves 30% of total ink usage when printed.

The typeface Futura appears on the cover. Commissioned by the Bauer type foundry, Futura was designed by Paul Renner in 1927. Though not actually associated with the Bauhaus design school, Renner supported the modernist approach espoused by the Bauhaus movement and designed Futura in that spirit.

The ampersands (&) used throughout the book come from Hoefler Text italic, a typeface designed by Jonathan Hoefler in 1991 for Apple Computer, Inc. The hand-drawn text on the front cover was inspired by Hoefler Text.